THE ARTIST'S TAO

44 Principles for an Artist's Life

SEAN STARR

PHOTOGRAPHY BY JENNIFER MOORE STARR

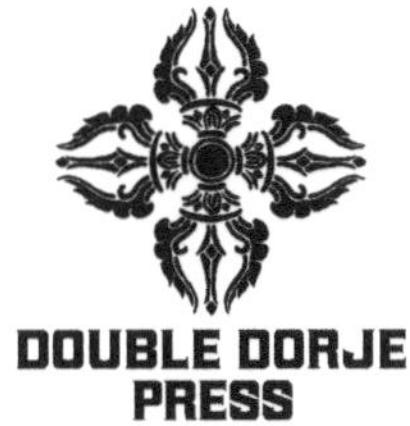

DOUBLE DORJE PRESS

Learn more at www.seanstarr.com

When I began writing the initial draft of "The Artist's Tao" in 2006, I had no idea
that this little book would traverse the globe, sparking inspiration among so
many other artists. Now, in 2024, I am encouraged to see how many of these
thoughts not only have endured but have evolved into pivotal principles shaping my
decisions as my career progressed. Like most artists, I have dedicated my life to the
pursuit of art, and engaging in discussions with fellow artists. This book is a
culmination of nearly four decades immersed in that creative process.

I have made some alterations to the wording, primarily by simplifying and distilling
the essence of each concept. However, the original intent remains intact, now presented
in a more digestible and memorable form. Additionally, this edition features a series
of photos by Jennifer Moore Starr capturing the interior of our studio in Calvert, Texas,
showcasing the materials employed in my artwork and a collection of items that serve
as sources of inspiration.

We trust that you will enjoy this new edition and discover inspiration and encouragement
within these ideas. The path of an artist has never been an easy one, yet it is a journey
I have never regretted.

May this book serve as a companion to aid you along your own artistic journey.

Sean Starr

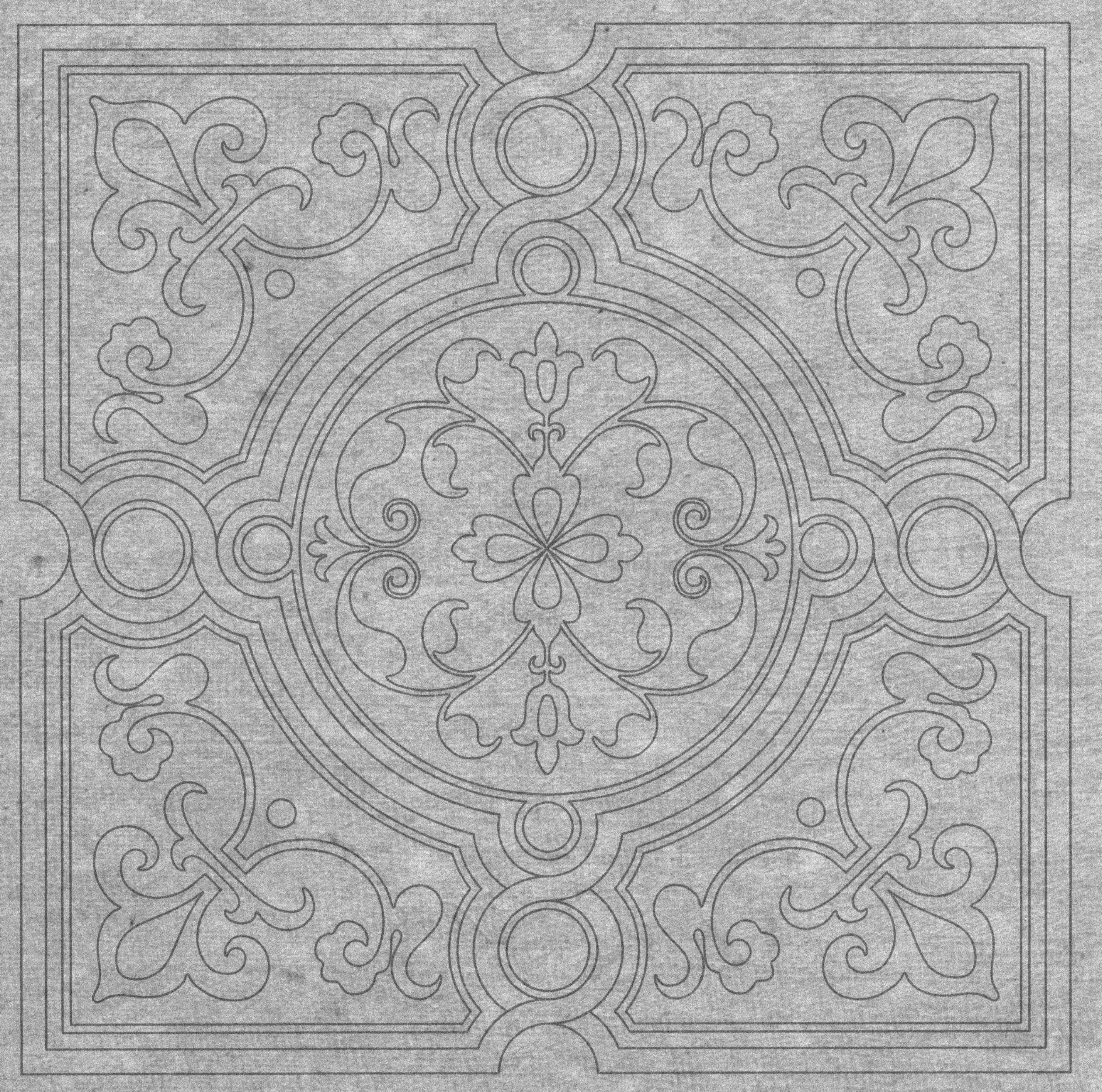

define yourself.

define your life as an artist
as you see fit,
not by society's definitions
of what an artist is.
do not allow anyone to confine you
with a stereotype.

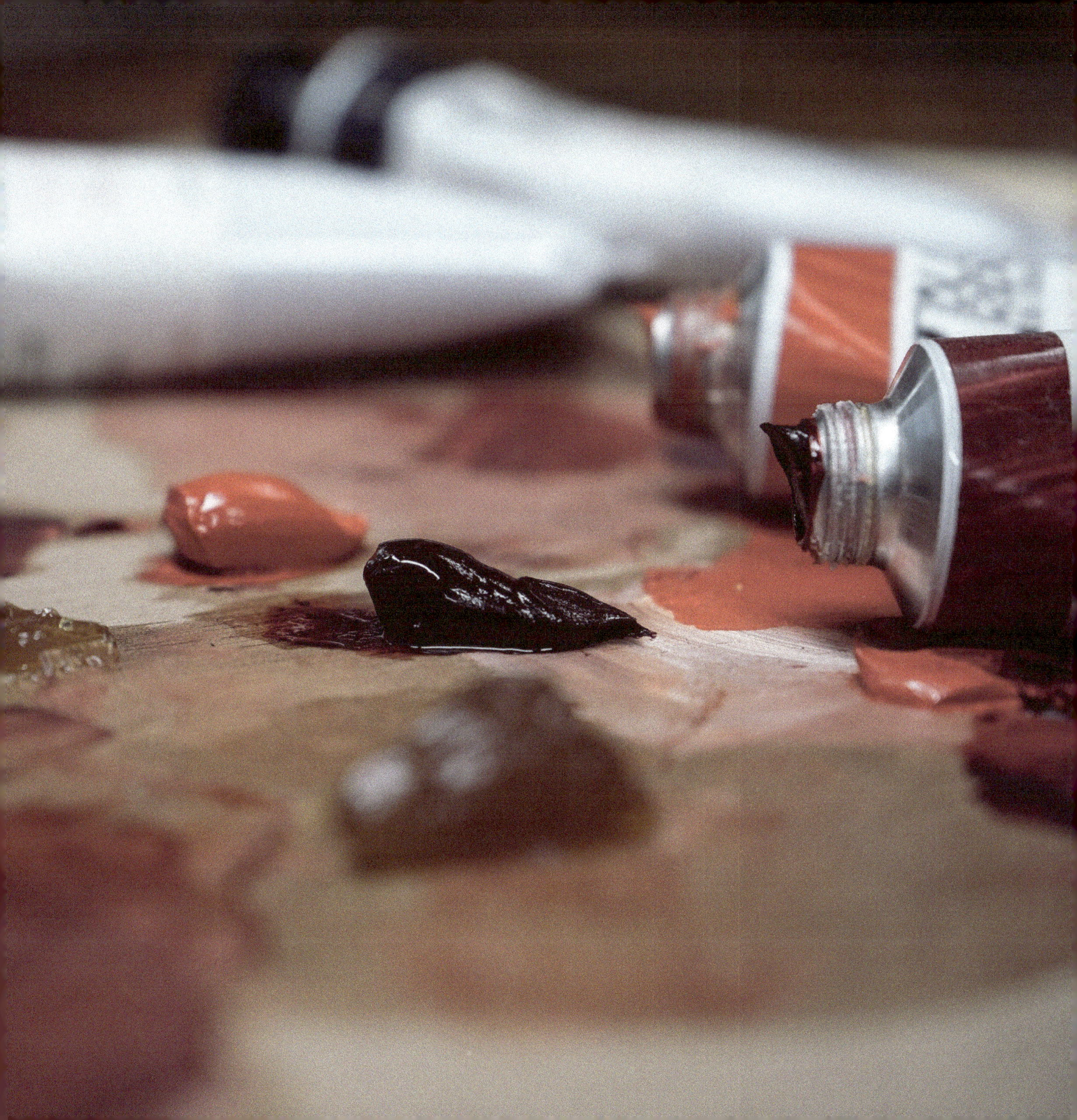

understand your role.

artists are the heart of the community.
although small, this is the part of the
community that ignites change.

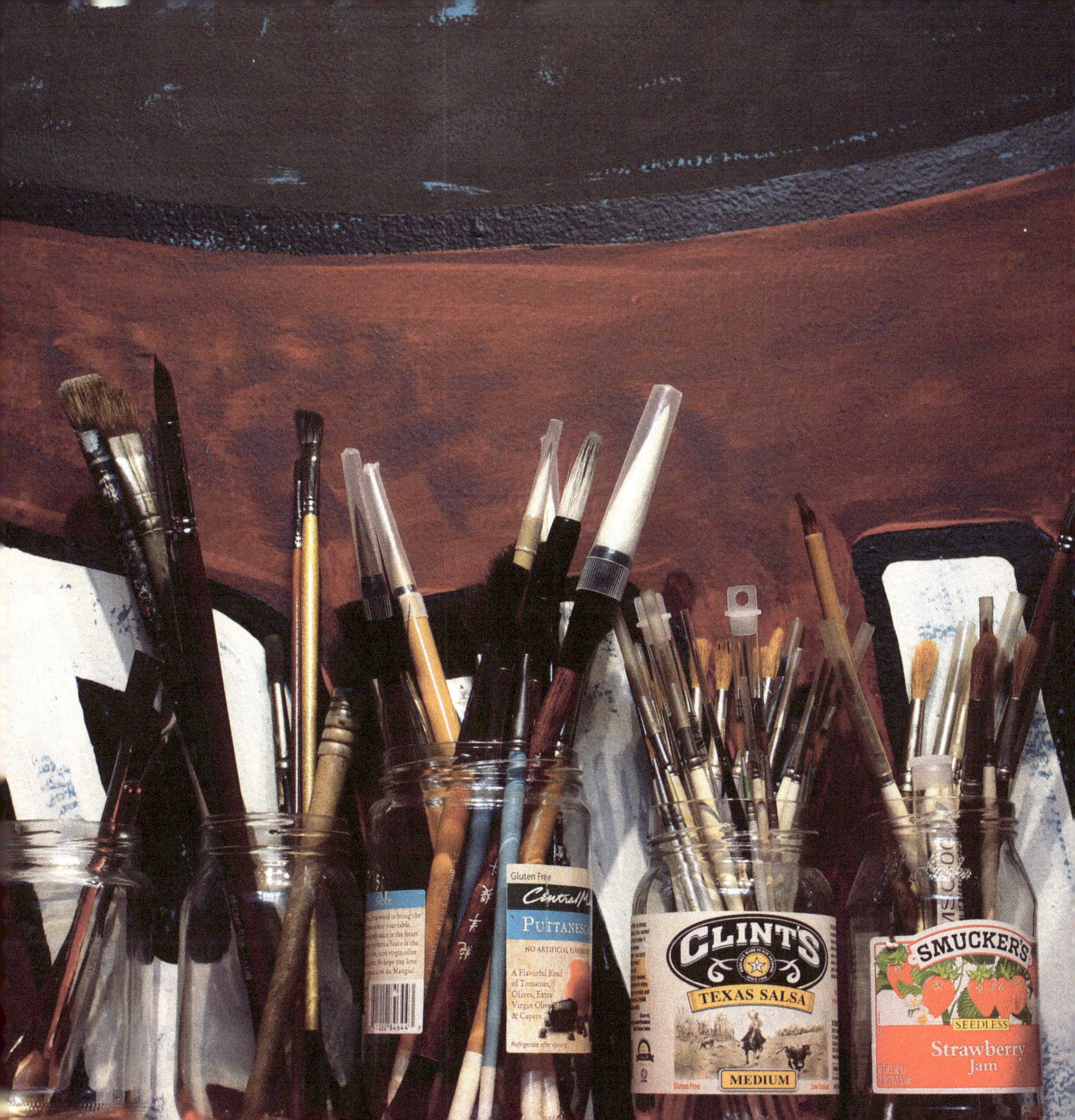

Gluten Free
Central M...
PUTTANESC...
NO ARTIFICIAL FLAVOR...
A Flavorful Blend
of Tomatoes,
Olives, Extra
Virgin Olives
& Capers
Refrigerate after opening
CLINT'S
TEXAS SALSA
MEDIUM
SMUCKER'S
SEEDLESS
Strawberry
Jam

be innovative.

embrace technology and build an audience.
the greatest achievement of any artist is to
communicate their ideas clearly.
figure out where you can be best heard.

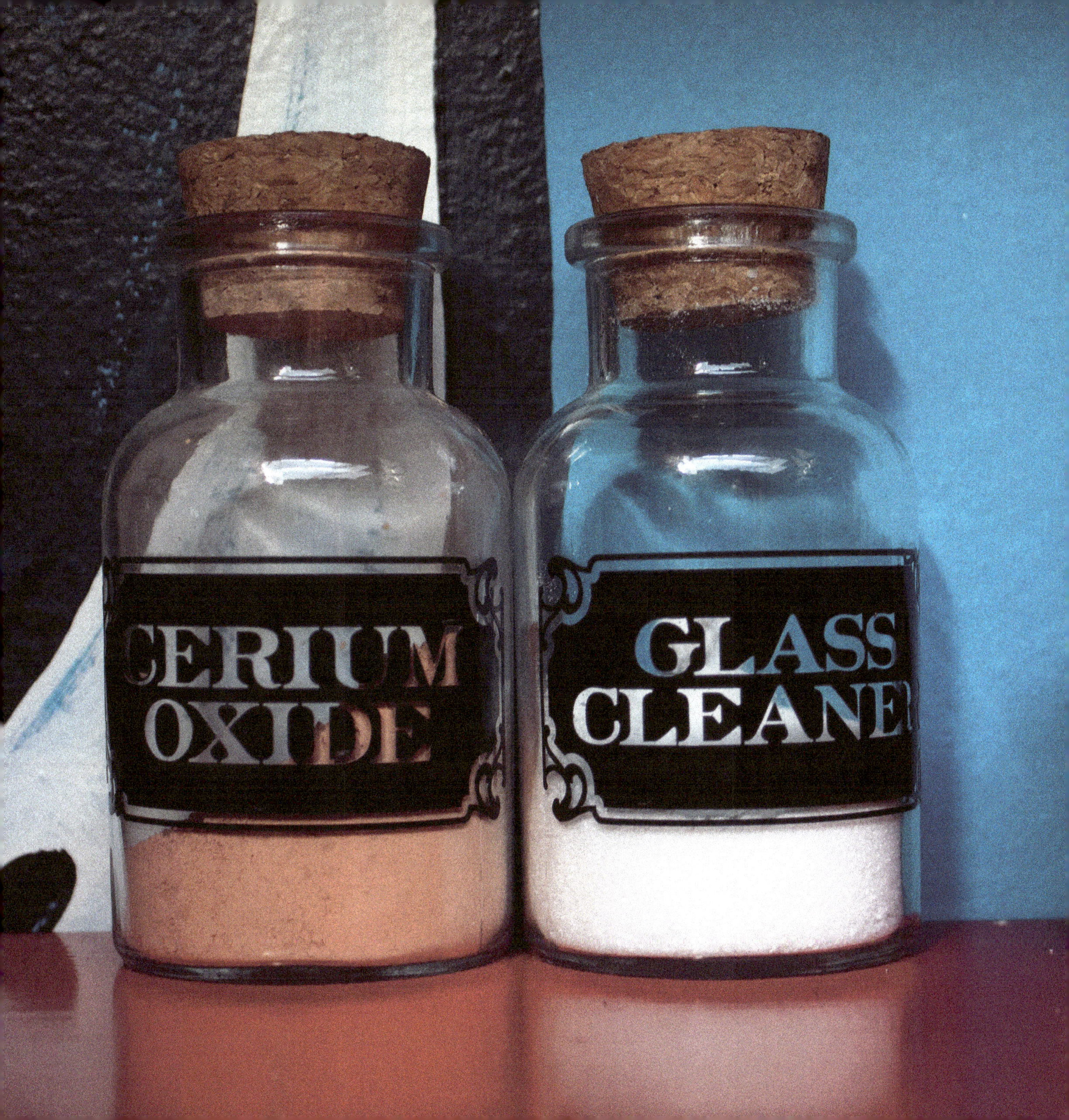

CERIUM
OXIDE

GLASS
CLEANER

honesty is key.

honesty demands strength.
it will expose things about yourself
that you do not want to see.
cultivate an appetite for honesty.

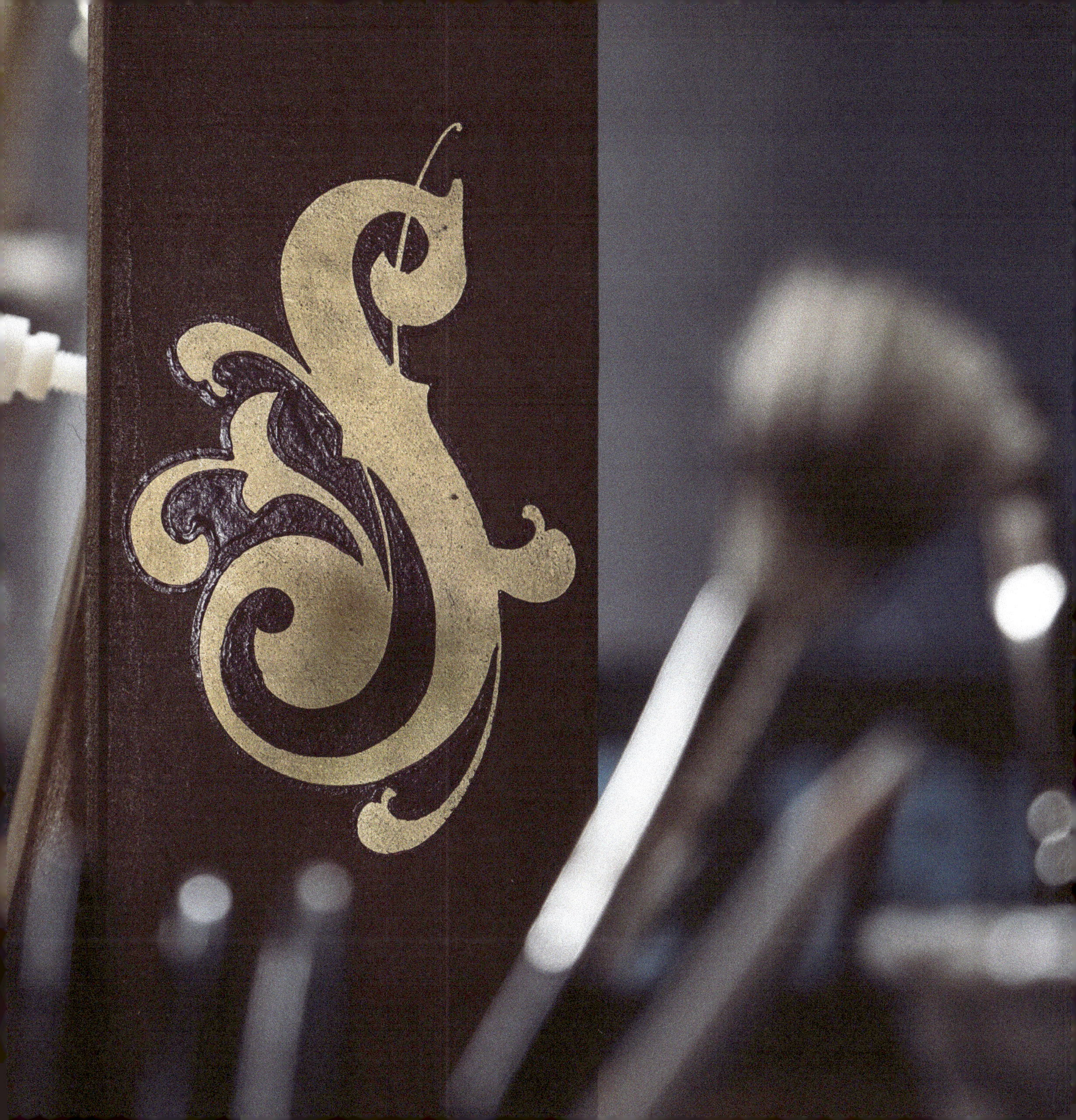

explore.

do not become attached
to one single means of expression.
do not trap yourself.

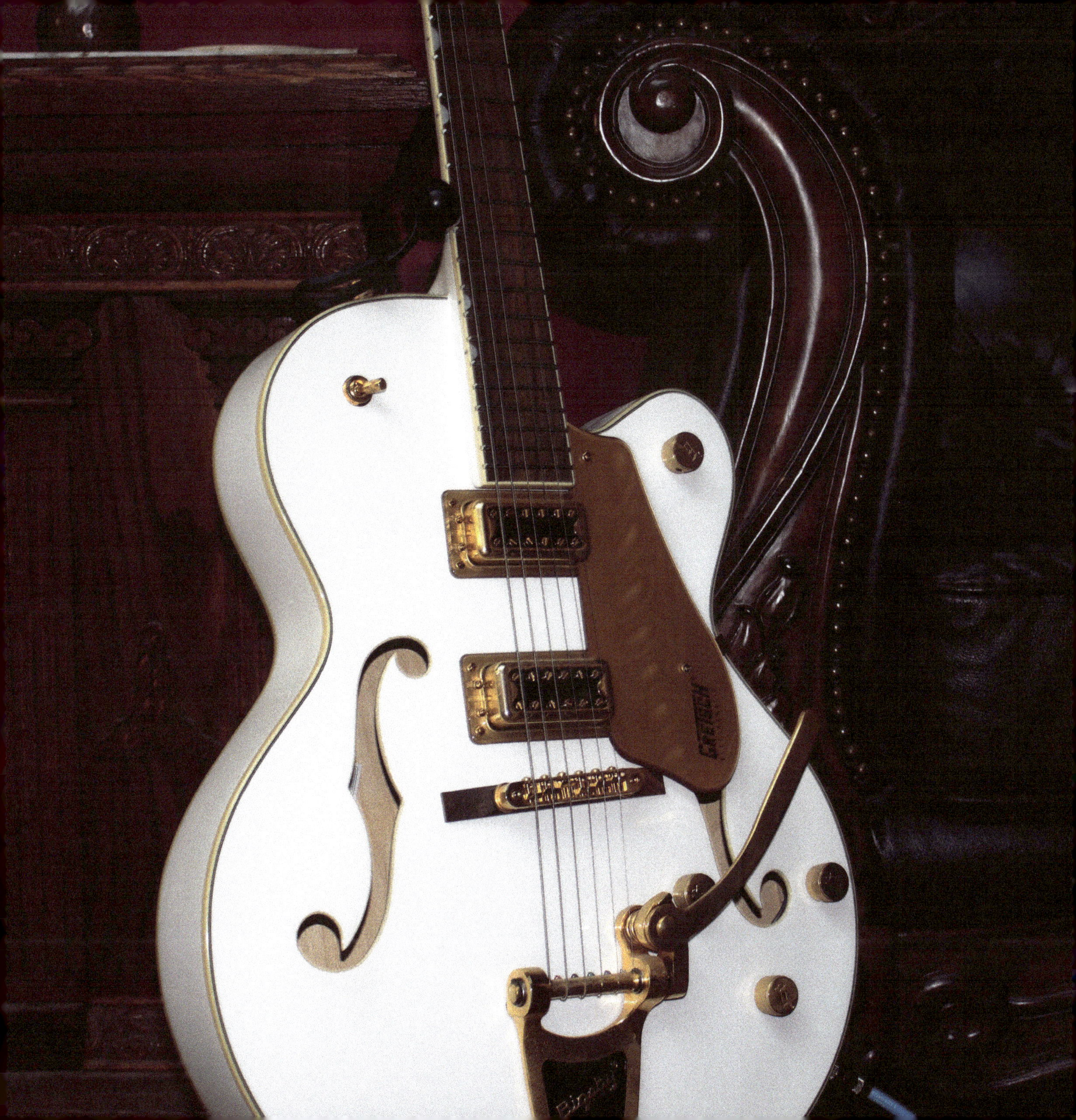

endurance.

endurance must be
cultivated to grow.
take a deep breath and
prepare for a long journey.

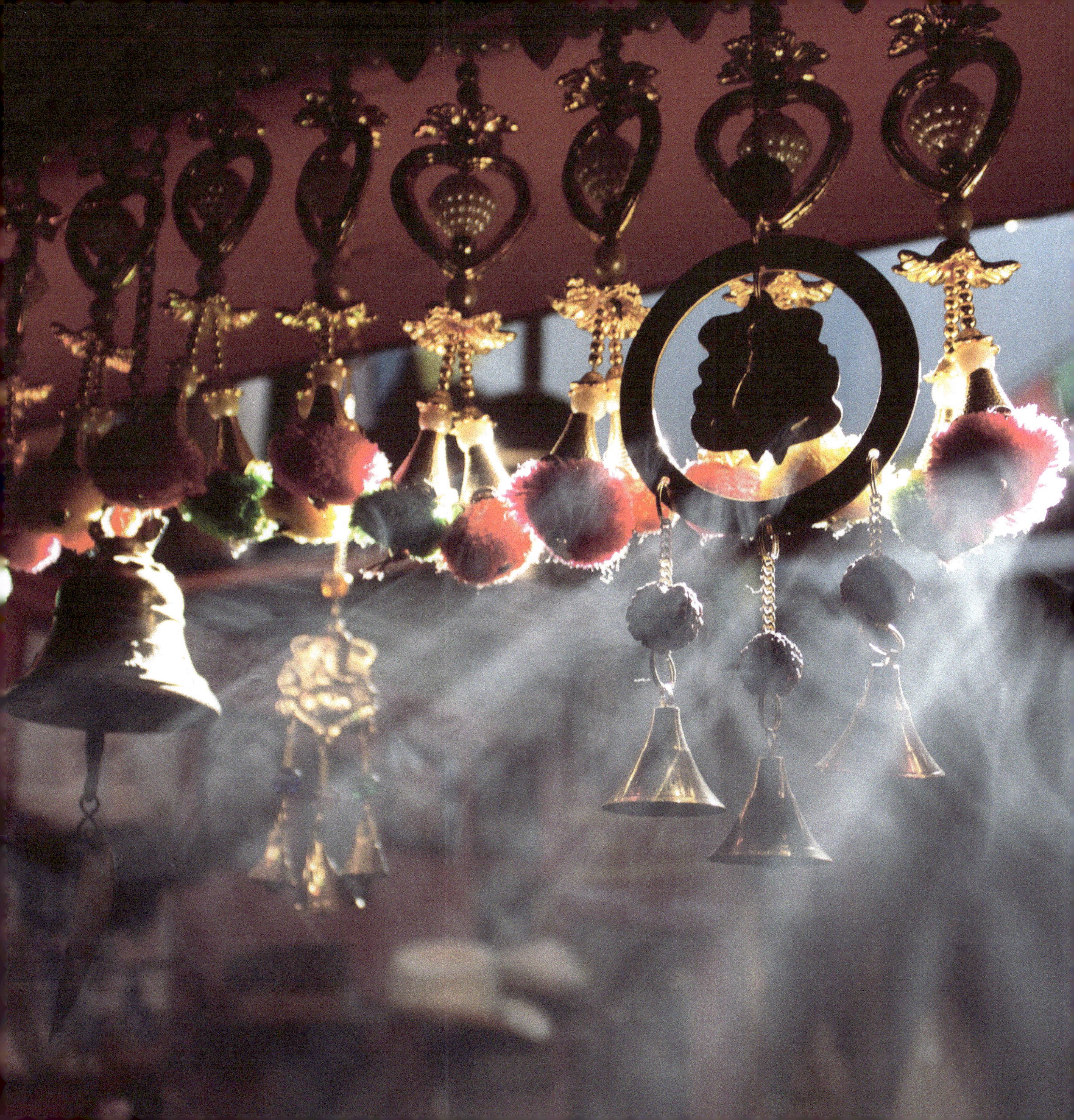

fight discouragement.

some people around you
will want you to fail.
your success may
reveal their shortcomings.
you cannot allow this
to alter your path.

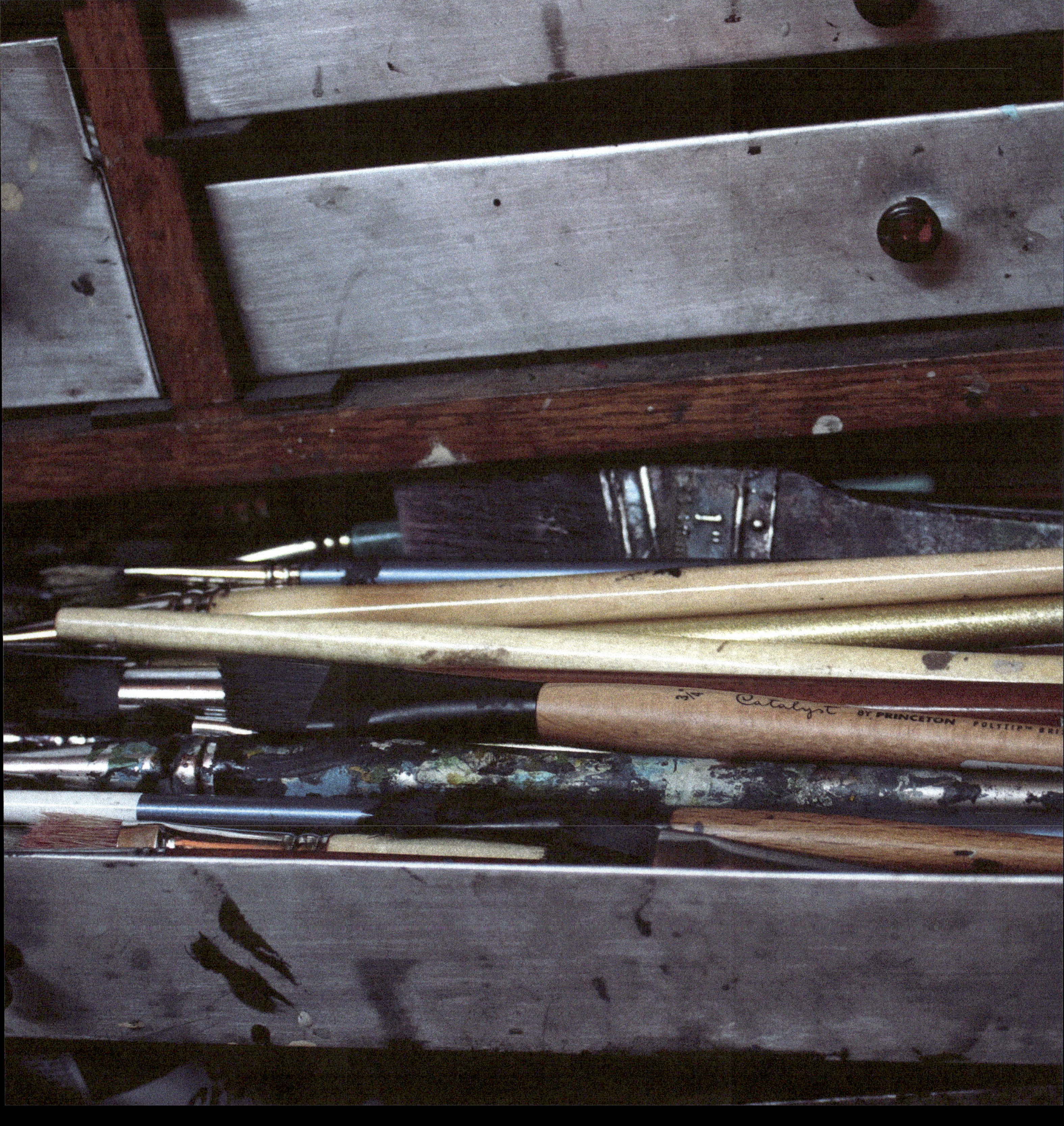
Catalyst
BY PRINCETON POLYTIP BRI

define your own success.

never measure the level of your success
as an artist by financial gain.
define what success means to you and
let that be your guide.

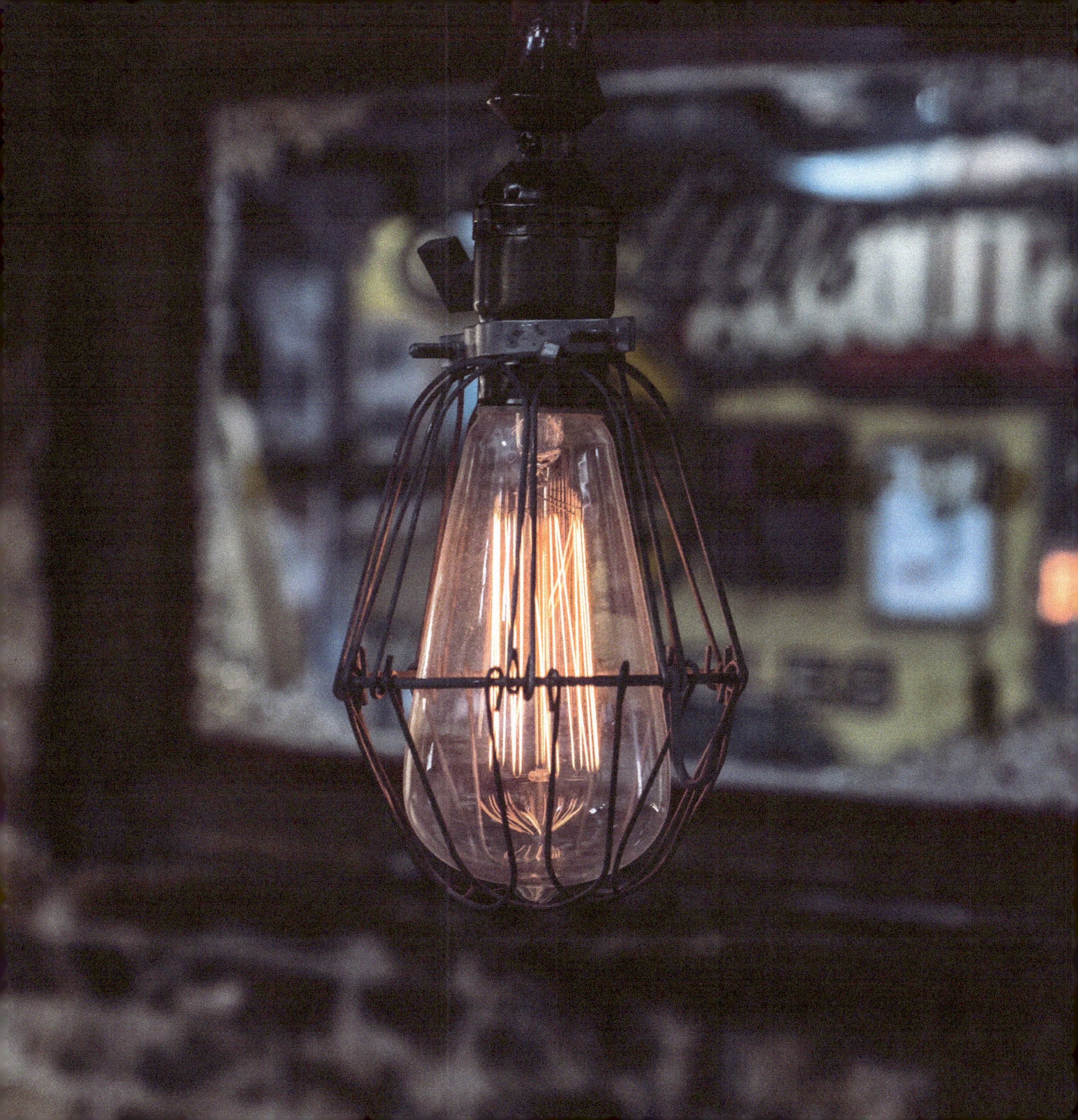

keep your integrity.

never alter your work
based on criticism.
never alter your work
based on commercial gain.

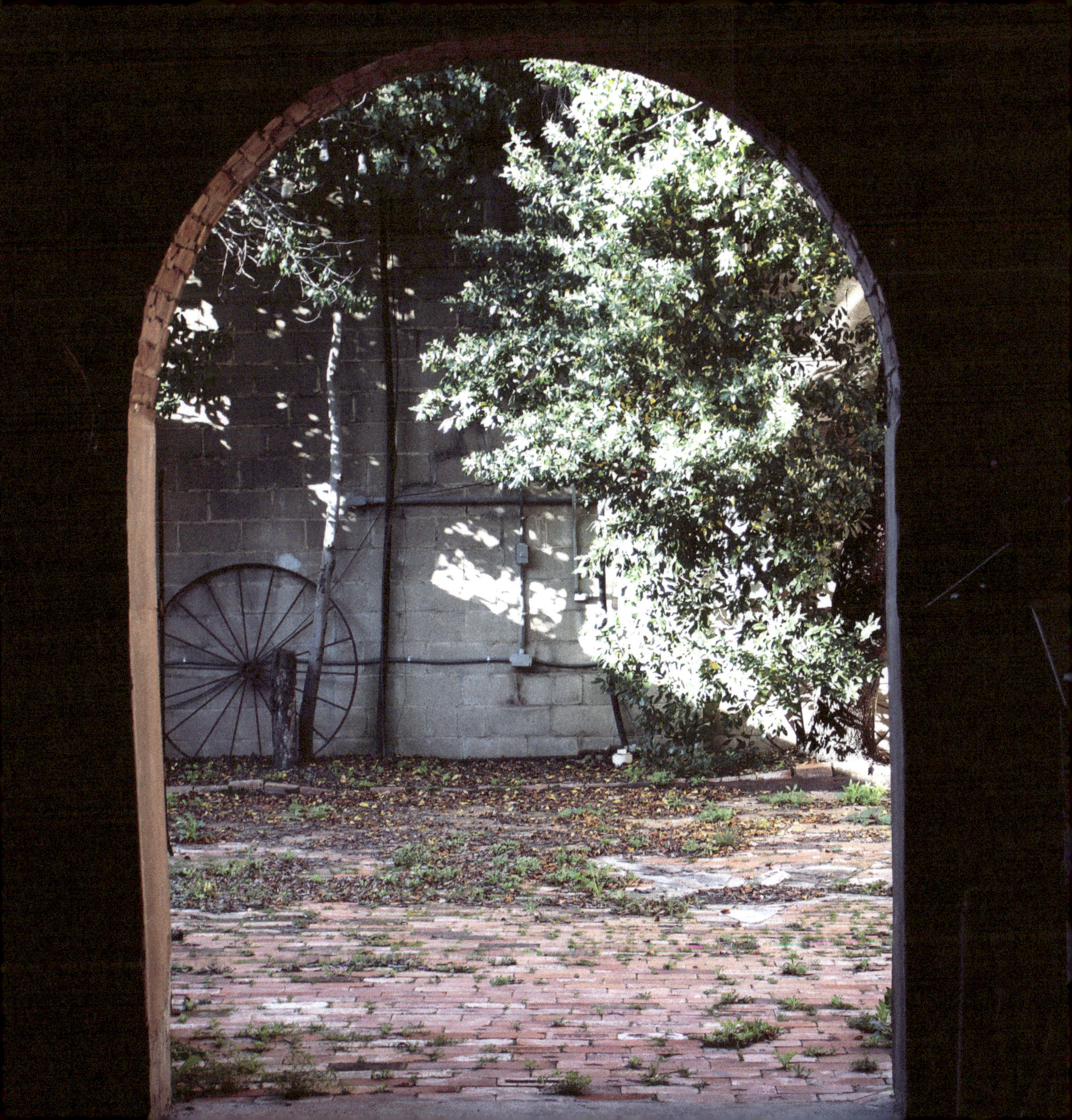

embrace your nature.

you are creative by nature.
although it is a generous idea,
not everyone else is driven creatively.

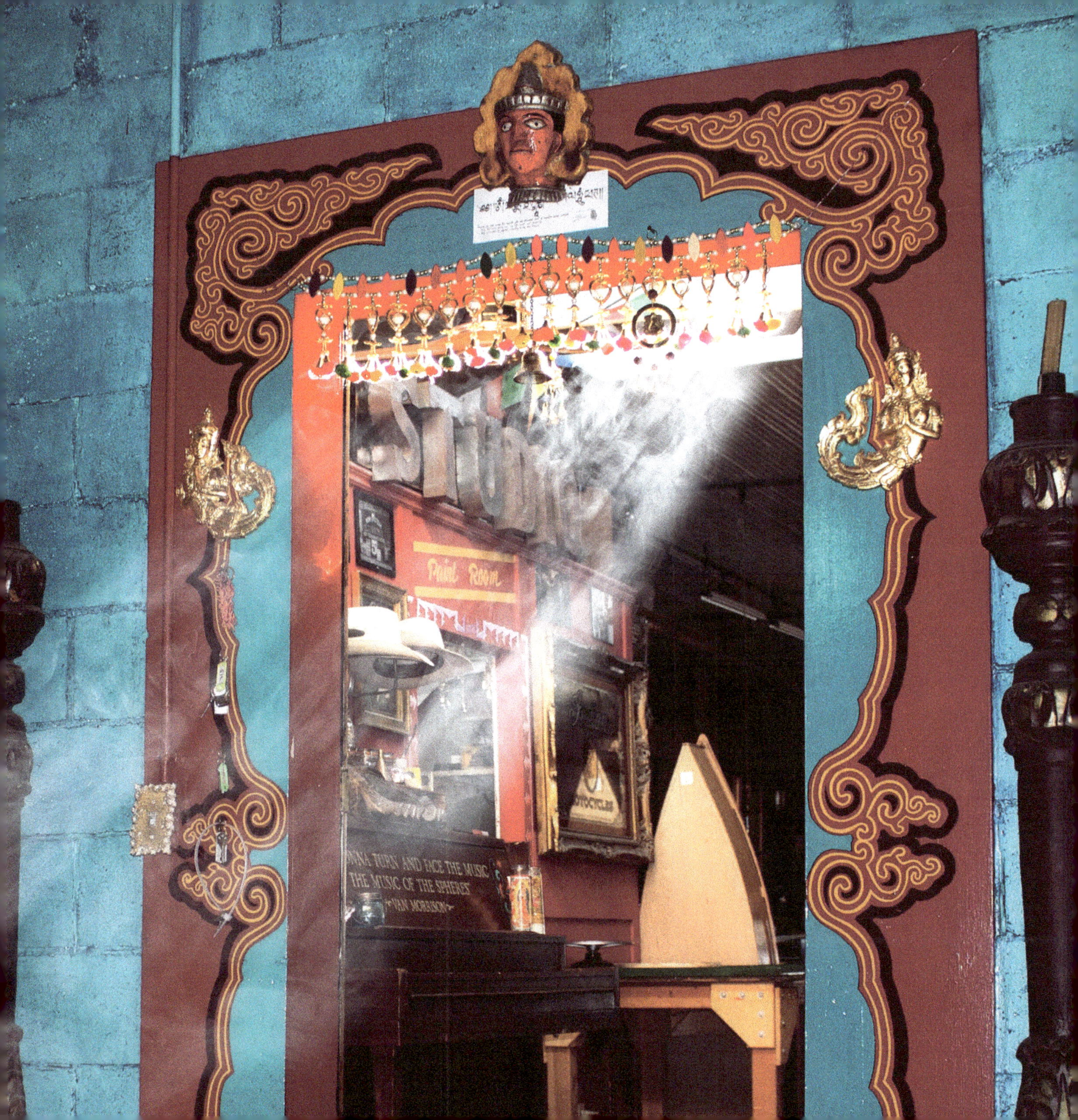
TURN AND FACE THE MUSIC
THE MUSIC OF THE SPHERES
~VAN MORRISON~
Print Room

make your contribution.

it is a strange world.
there are others working on expressing the
exact same thing as you are right now.
look at your work as a contribution
to something much larger.

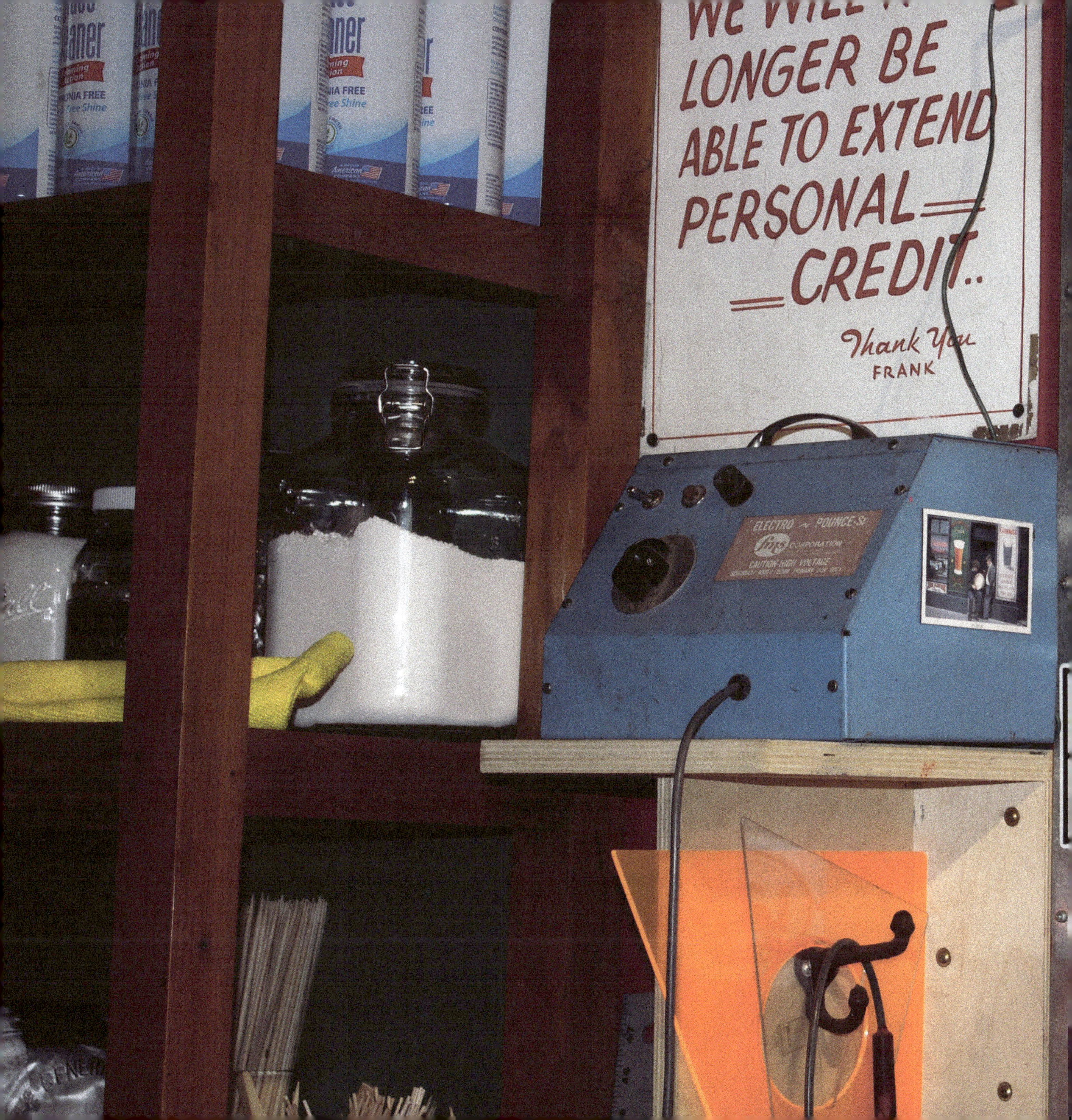

WE WILL N
LONGER BE
ABLE TO EXTEND
PERSONAL
CREDIT..
Thank You
FRANK
ELECTRO ~ POUNCE-S
Corporation
CAUTION-HIGH VOLTAGE

get persistent.

it may be years down the road
before you can see measurable progress
in your work or what you define as success.

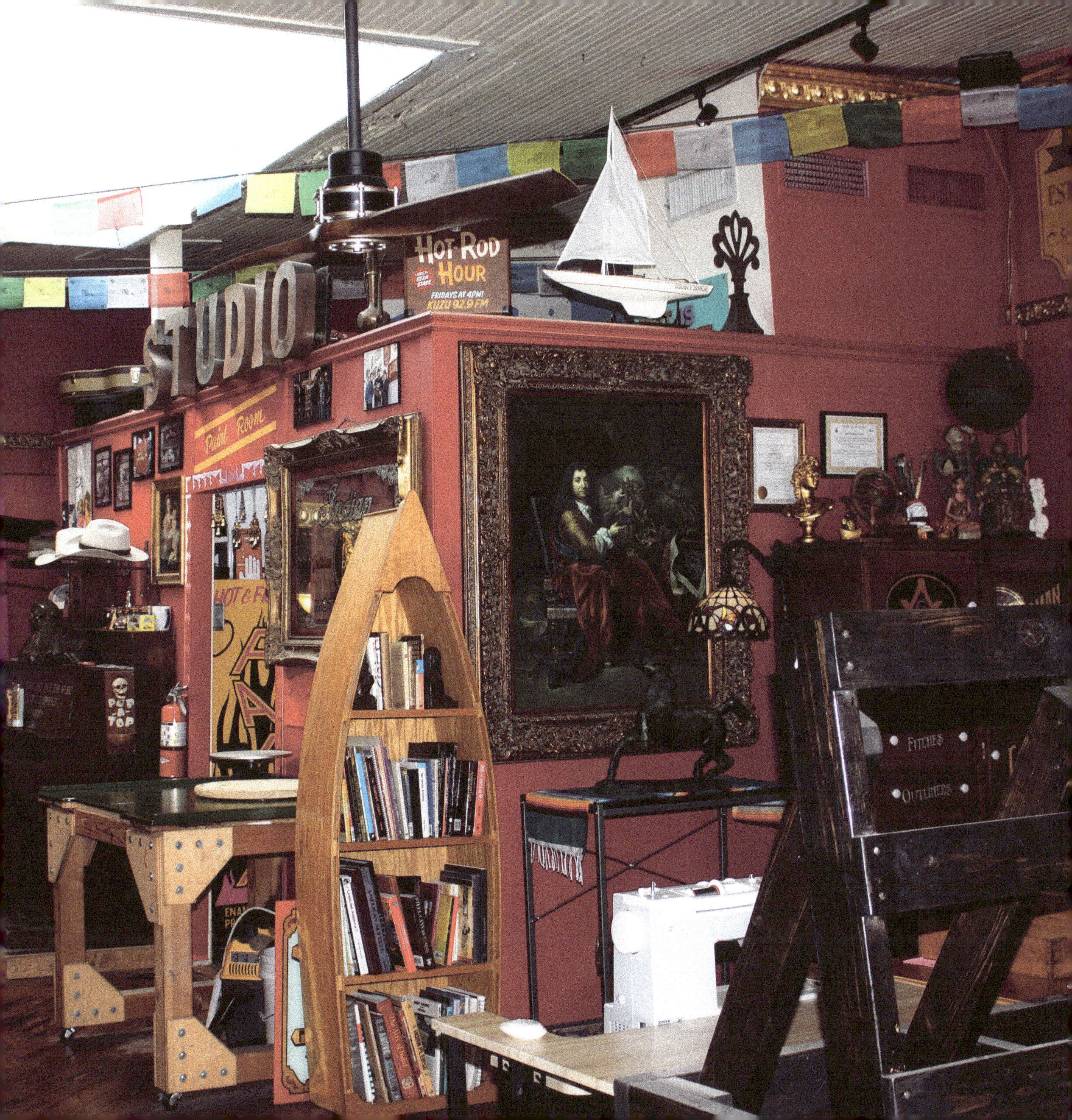

STUDIO
HOT ROD HOUR
FRIDAYS AT 4PM
KUZU 92.9 FM
Paint Room
Indian
FITCHES
OUTLINERS

embrace unity.

you are connected to every
single person in your community.
they say aspen groves can
cover dozens of acres of land,
yet are one single organism.

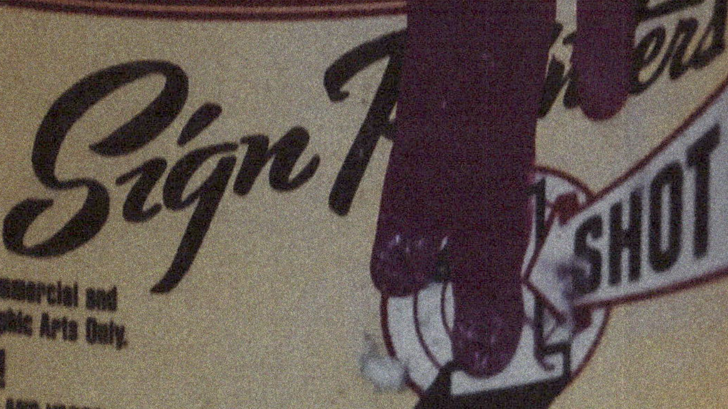

Sign Painters
SHOT
For Professional, Commercial and Industrial Use in Graphic Arts Only.
DANGER!
COMBUSTIBLE LIQUID AND VAPOR.
VAPOR HARMFUL. HARMFUL
OR FATAL IF SWALLOWED.
PAINT PEINTURE
LETTERING ENAMEL
164-L DARK MAGENTA
1 US HALF PINT

keep your balance.

seek balance in all your habits.
enjoy your wine and song,
but temper it with
a developed work ethic.

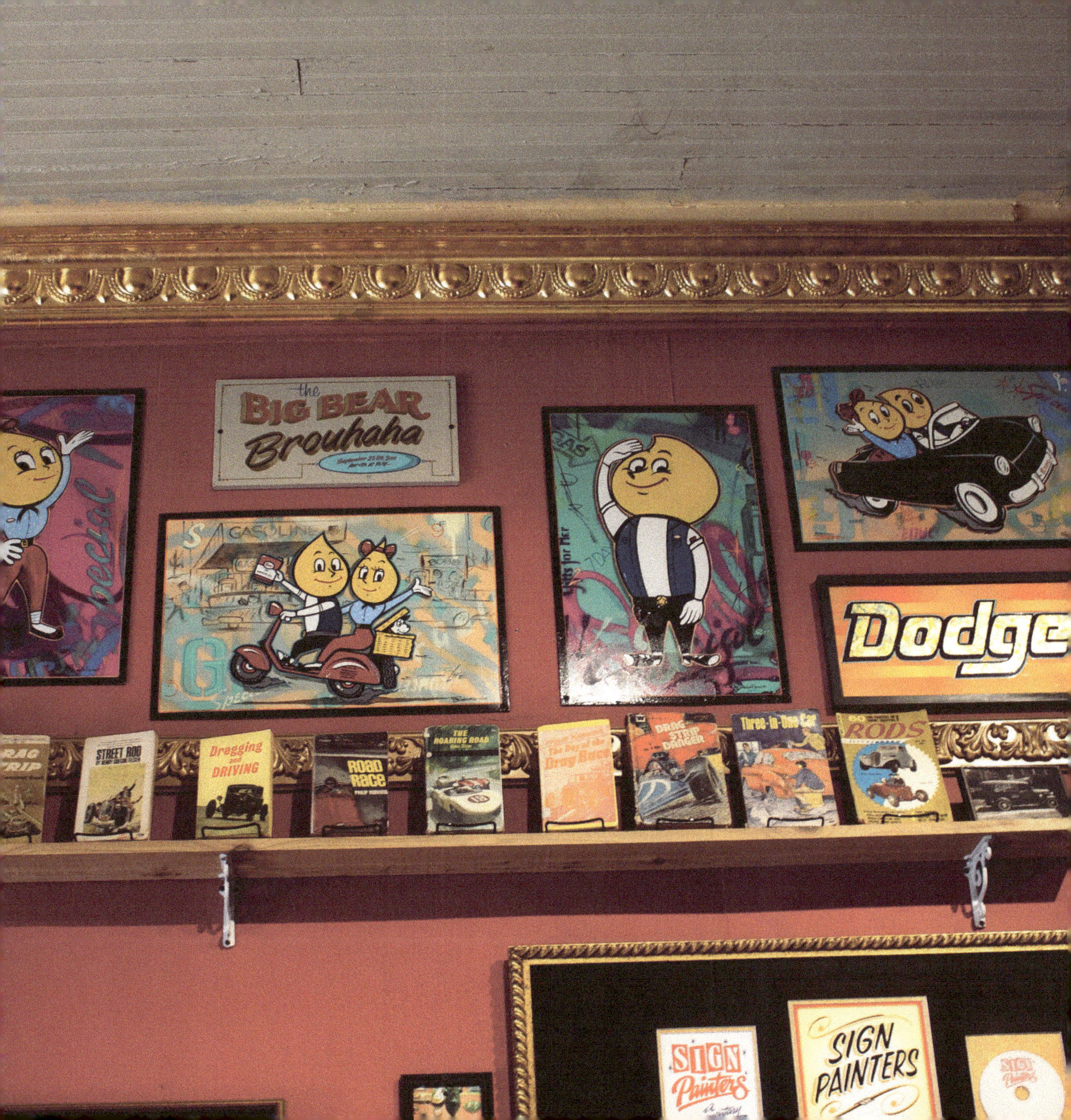

the
BIG BEAR
Brouhaha
Dodge
Special
GASOLINE
STREET ROD
Dragging and DRIVING
ROAD RACE
THE ROARING ROAD
DRAG STRIP DANGER
Three-in-One Car
RODS
SIGN Painters
SIGN PAINTERS

ignore the mythology.

do not invest in the mythology
of what defines an artist.
there is no need
to encourage or create
hardships to fuel your work.

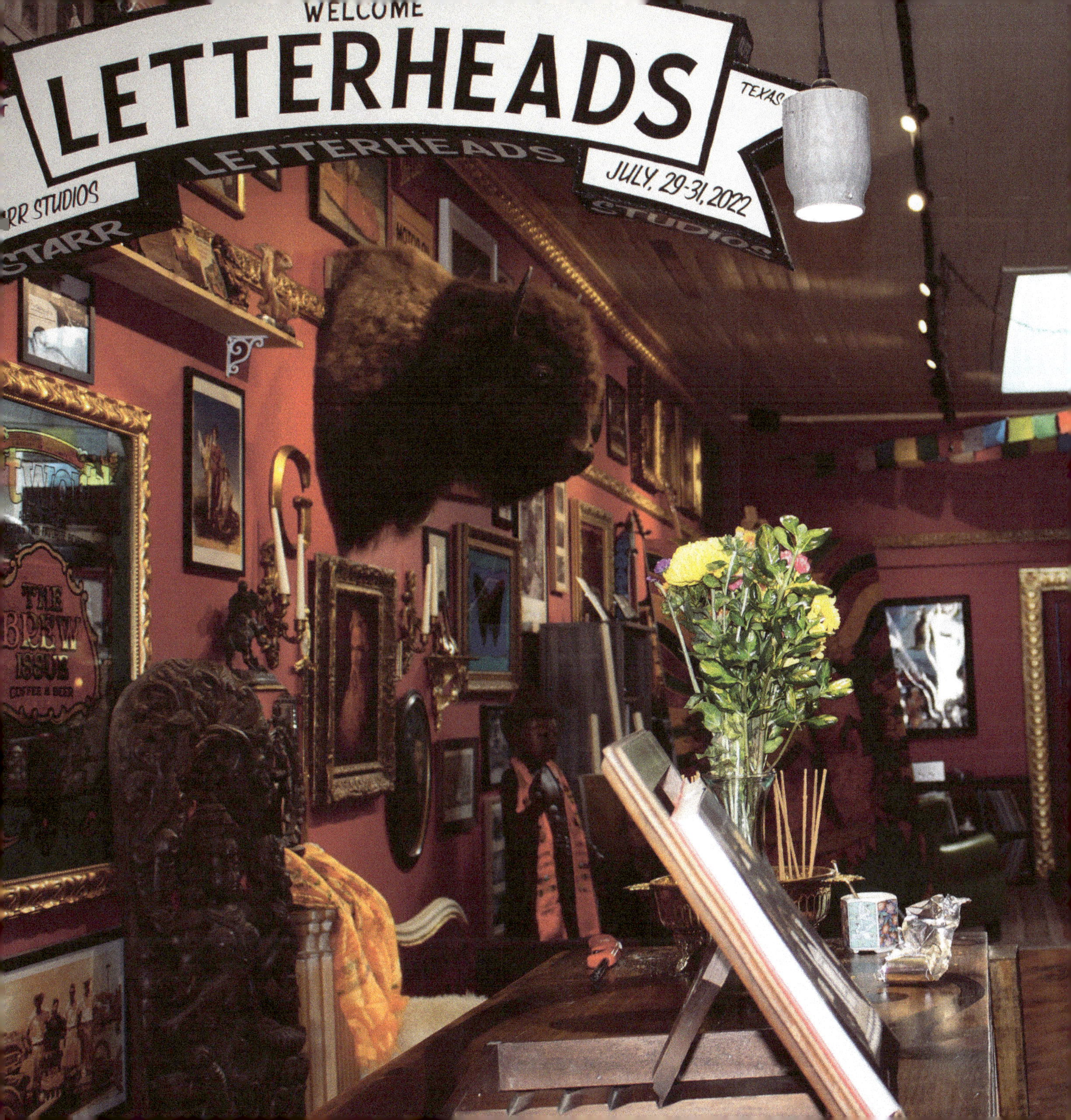

WELCOME
LETTERHEADS
TEXAS
JULY, 29-31, 2022
LETTERHEADS
STARR STUDIOS
STARR
STUDIOS

surrender.

make your decisions, and follow them through,
just understand that you cannot predetermine
the results of your choices.
stop seeking control.

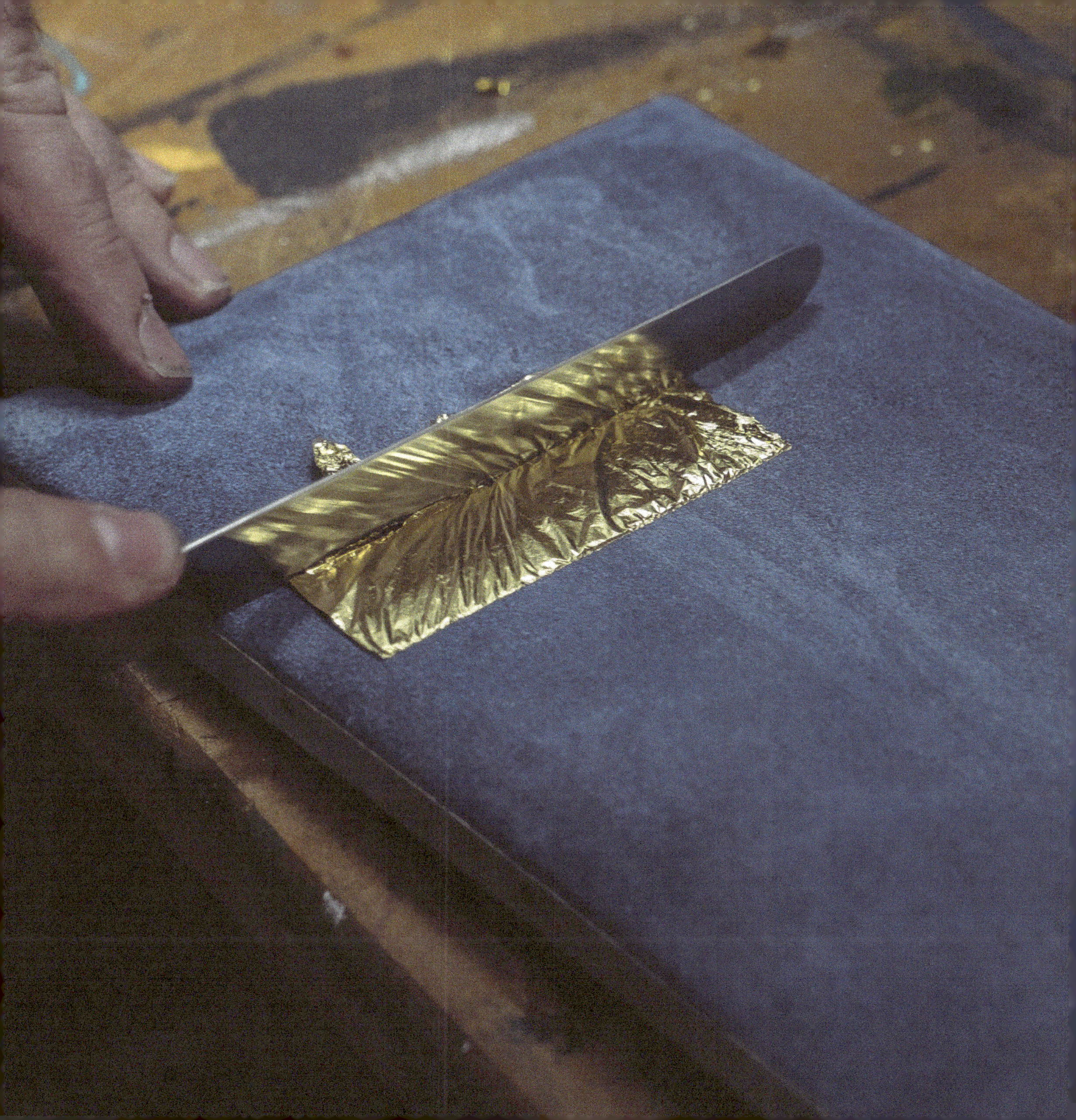

follow the work.

do not force anything.
your work knows better than you
which way it wants to go.

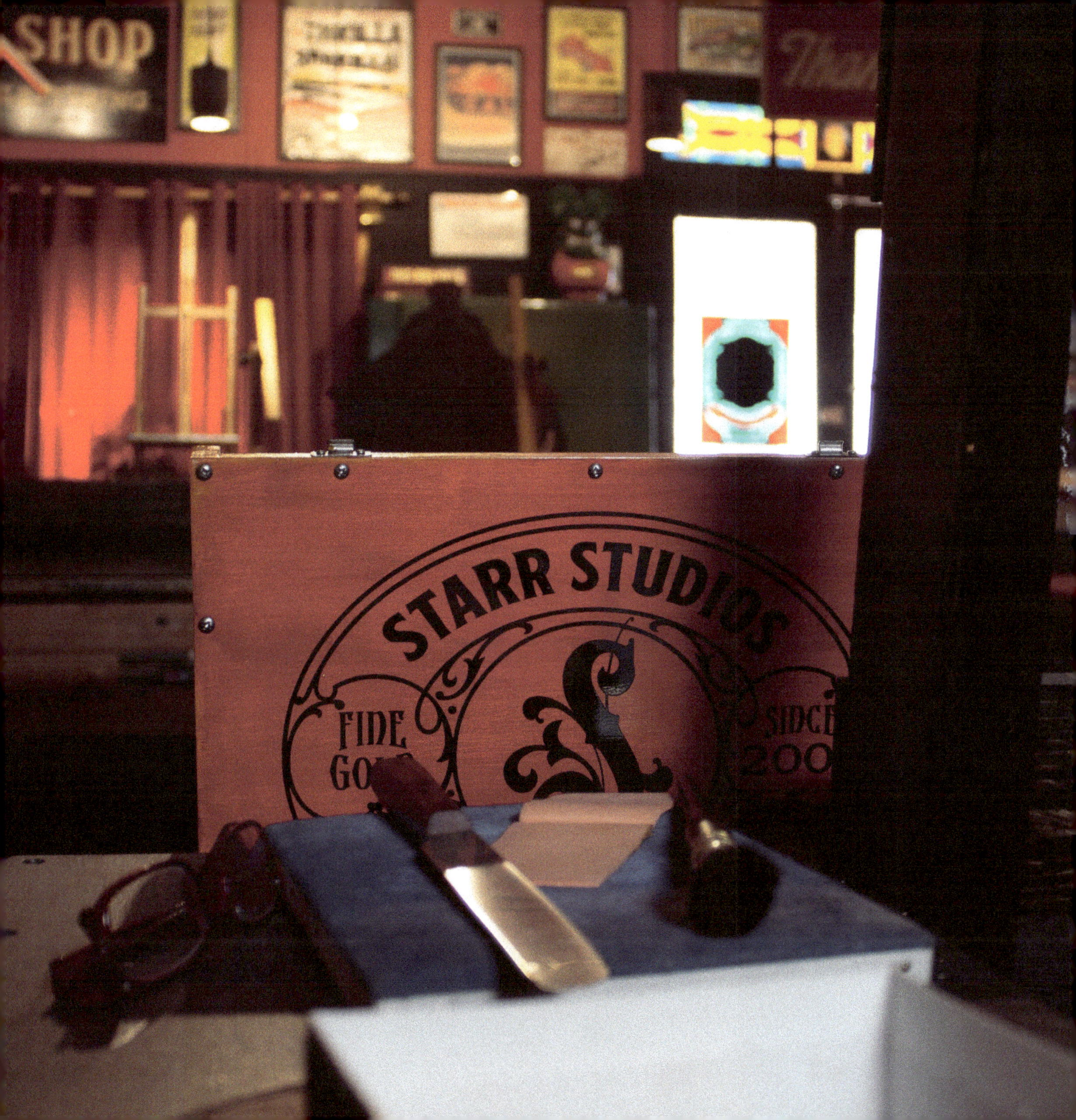

SHOP
STARR STUDIOS
FINE
GOLD
SINCE
200

be present.

create something beautiful every day.
value each day as special and unique.
obsession with past failures
or future desires robs you of the
magnificence of today.

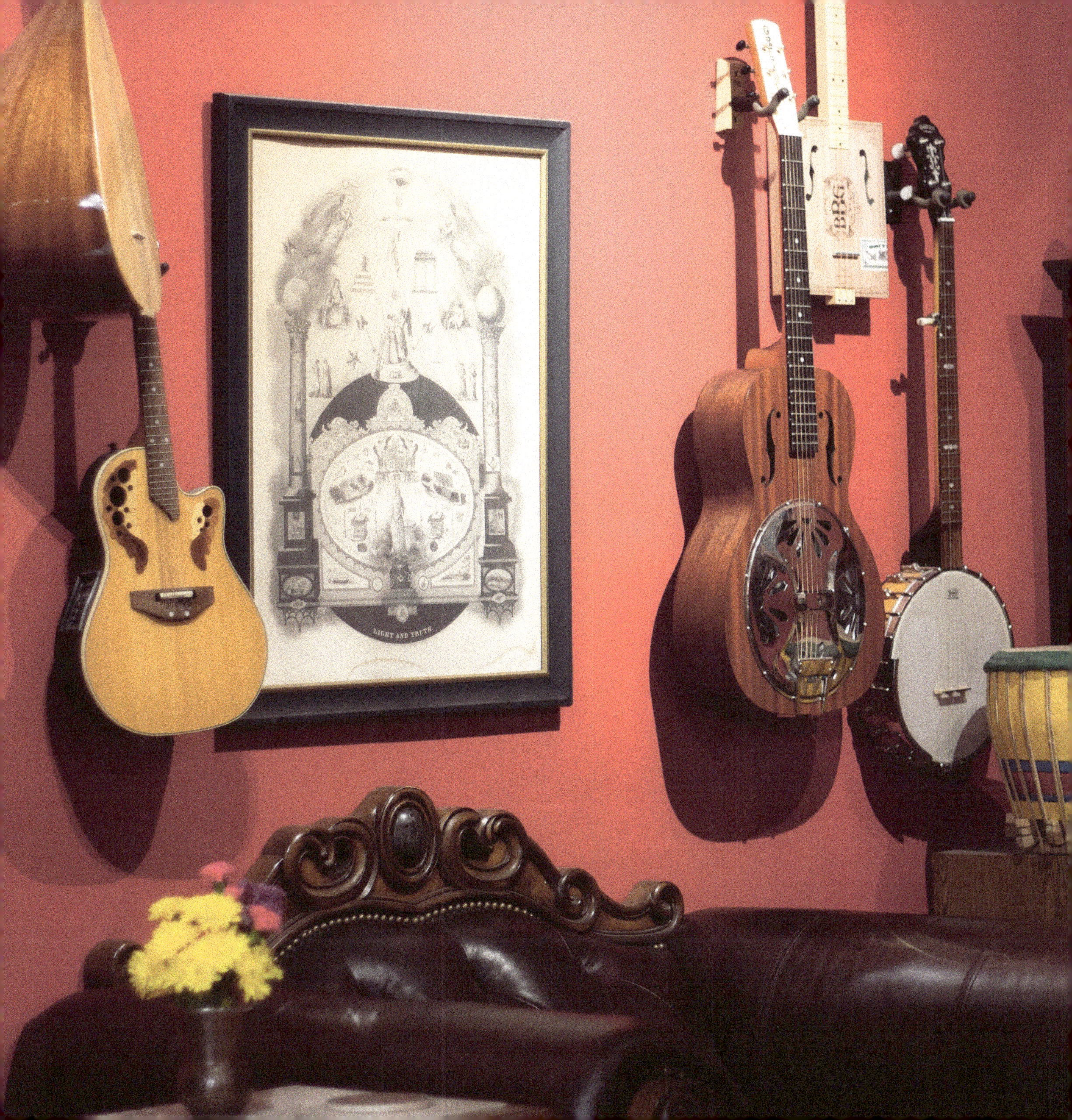
BBG
LIGHT AND TRUTH

ignore your doubts.

silence your doubts.
learn to ignore them like the sound of
your neighbor's barking dog.
you cannot be your own critic.

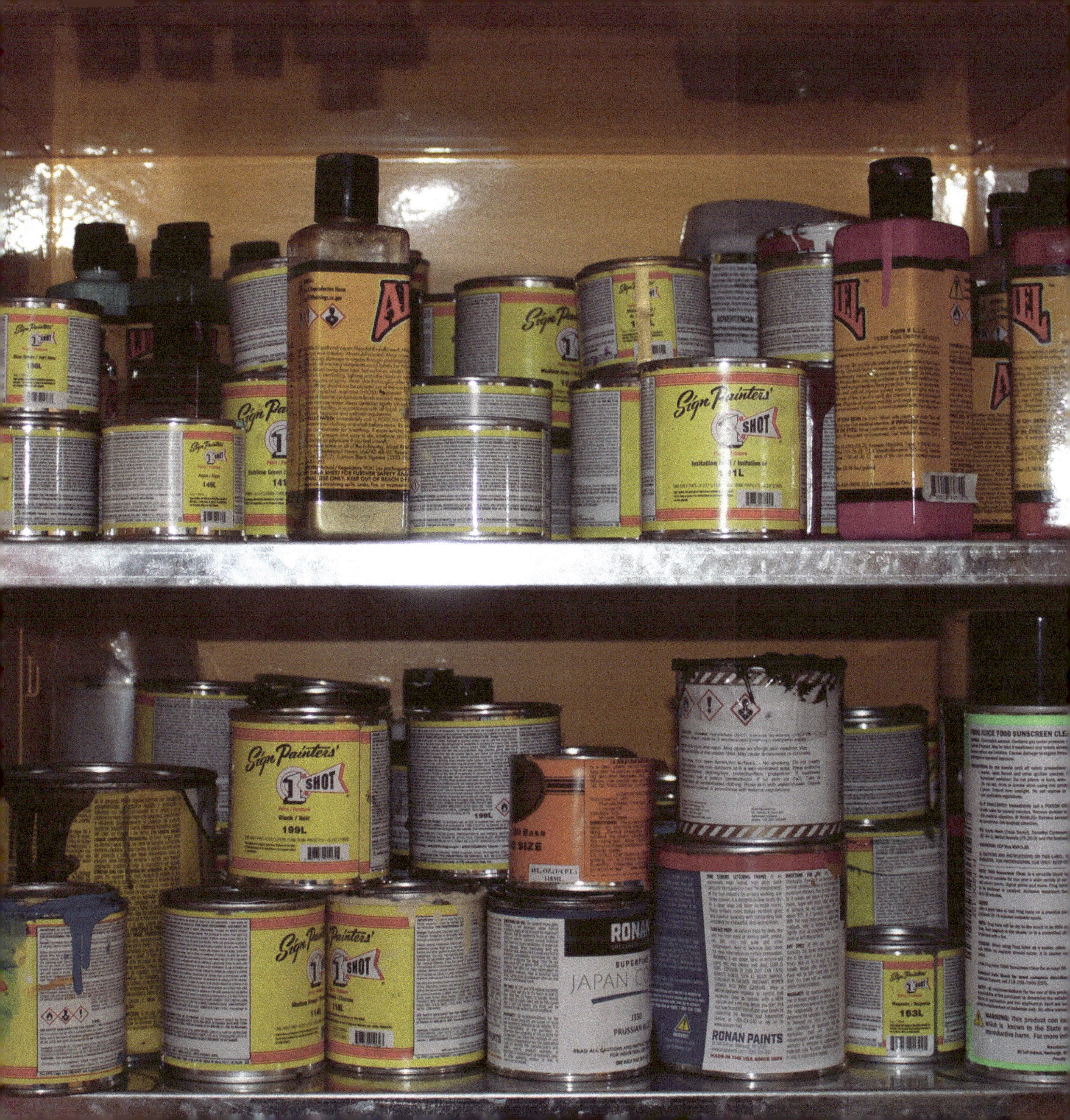

Sign Painters'
1 SHOT
Sign Painters'
1 SHOT
Imitation Gold / Imitation or
Sign Painters'
1 SHOT
Black / Noir
199L
Sign Painters'
1 SHOT
Prussian Blue
116L
163L
149L
141L
150L
ADVERTENCIA
RONAN
SUPERFINE
JAPAN CO
1350
PRUSSIAN BLUE
RONAN PAINTS
MADE IN THE USA SINCE 1886
READ ALL CAUTIONS AND
FOR INDUSTRIAL USE
Base
SIZE
4 FL. OZ. (1/4 PT.)
118ML
FROG JUICE 7000 SUNSCREEN CLEAR
WARNING: This product can
which is known to the State of
reproductive harm. For more in

let your inhibitions go.

when you find yourself
creating without inhibition,
this is the sweet spot.
learn to recognize it.

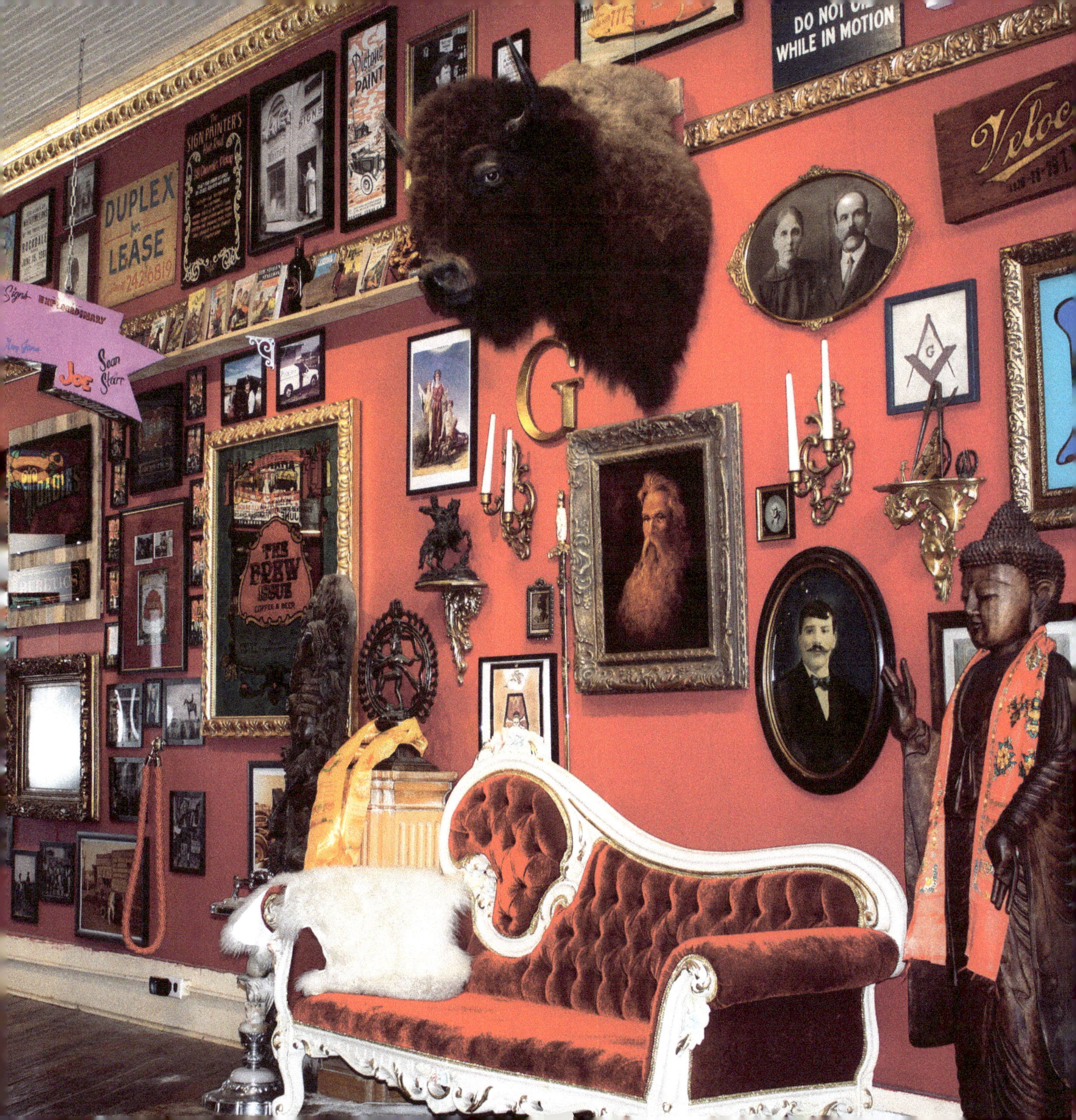

DO NOT USE
WHILE IN MOTION
DUPLEX
for
LEASE
PAINT
Sean Starr
Joe
THE
BREW
ISSUE
COFFEE & BEER
G

kick limitations to the curb.

destroy your self made limitations.
never limit yourself.

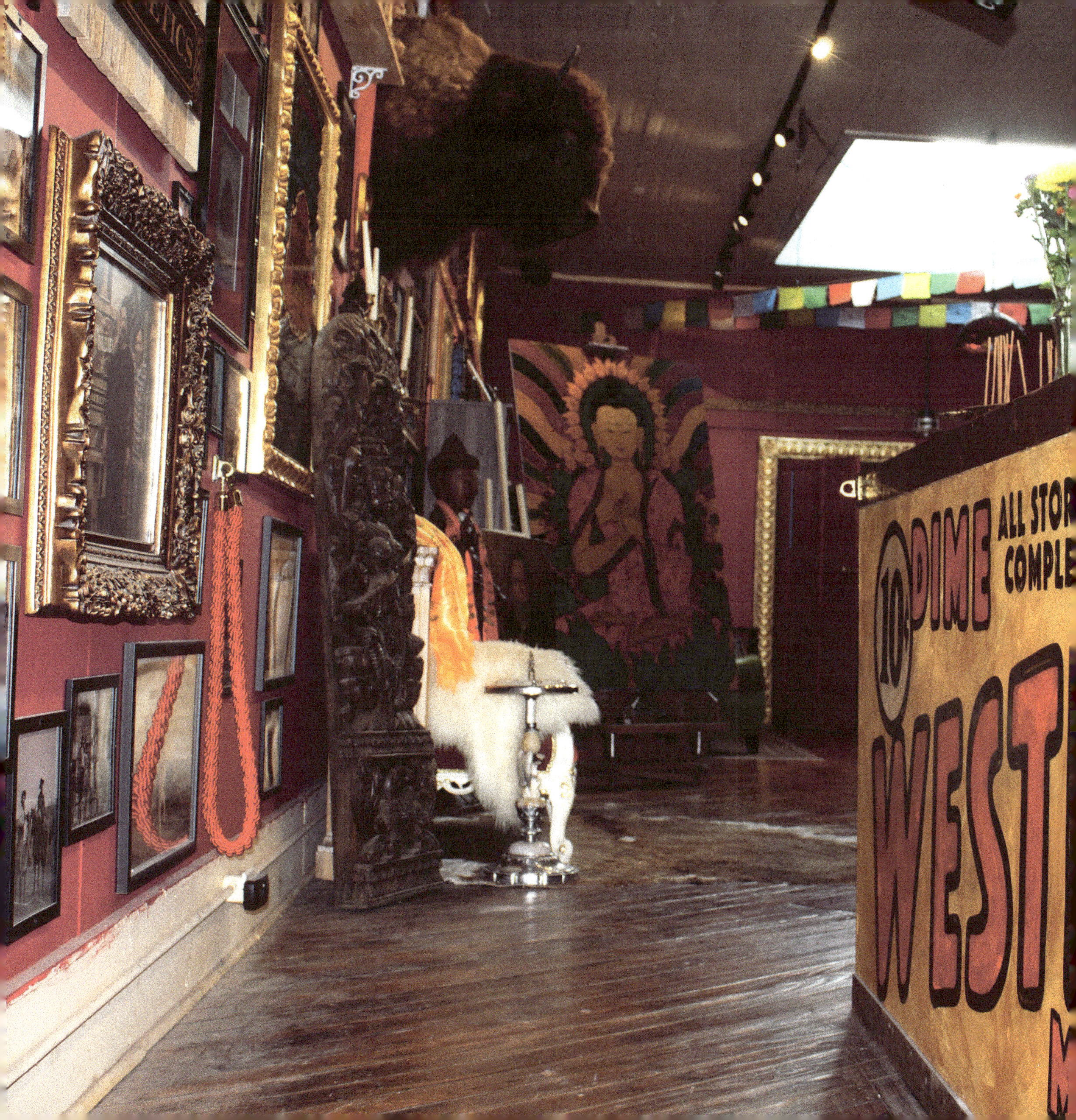

10¢ DIME ALL STOR COMPLE
WEST

become a guide.

help others explore their
own creativity, you will help them
and you will learn more about yorself.

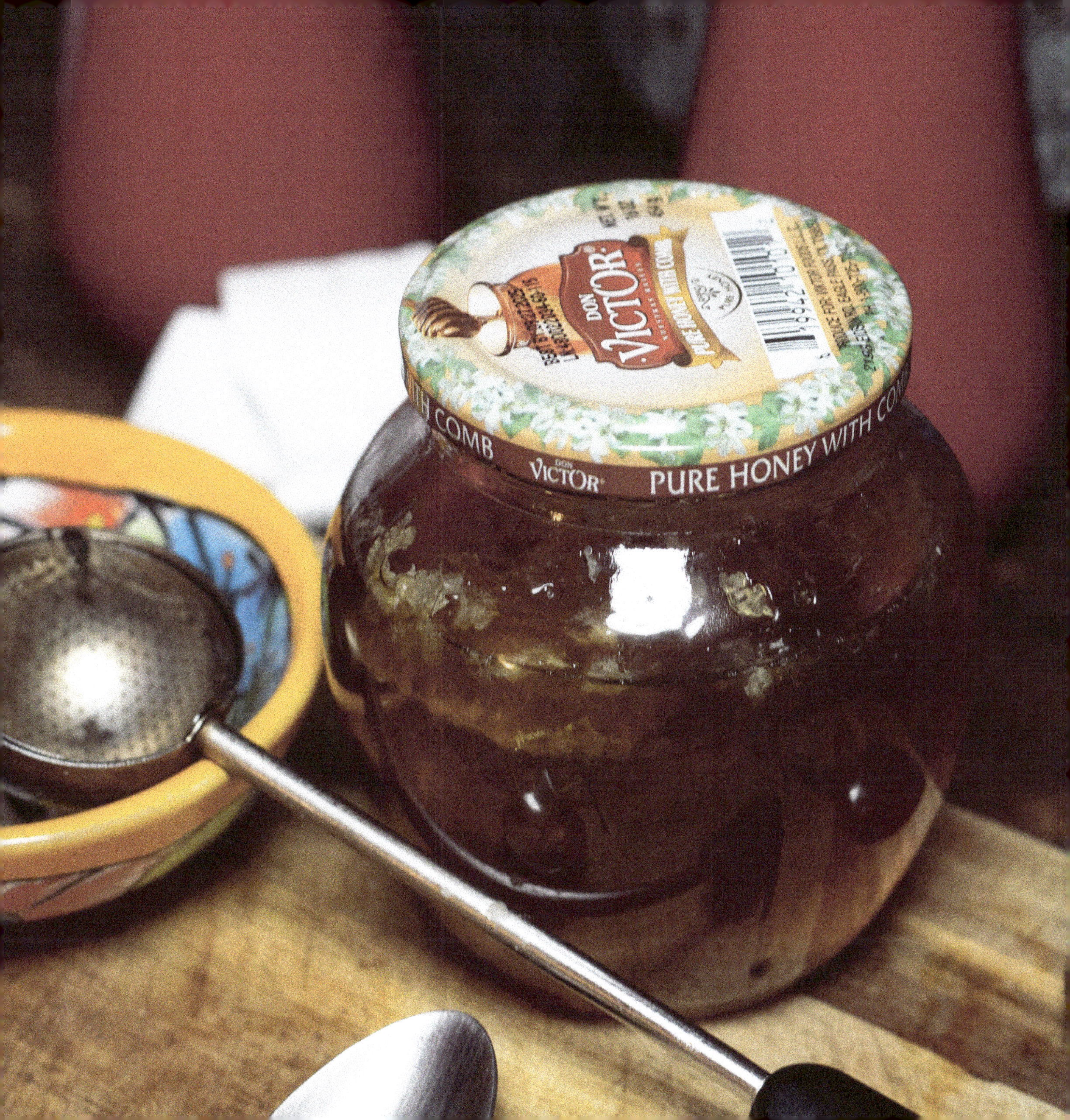
DON VICTOR
PURE HONEY WITH COMB
DON VICTOR
PURE HONEY WITH COMB

stay humble.

do not elevate yourself.
an artist is just as essential as
an electrician,
plumber or auto mechanic.

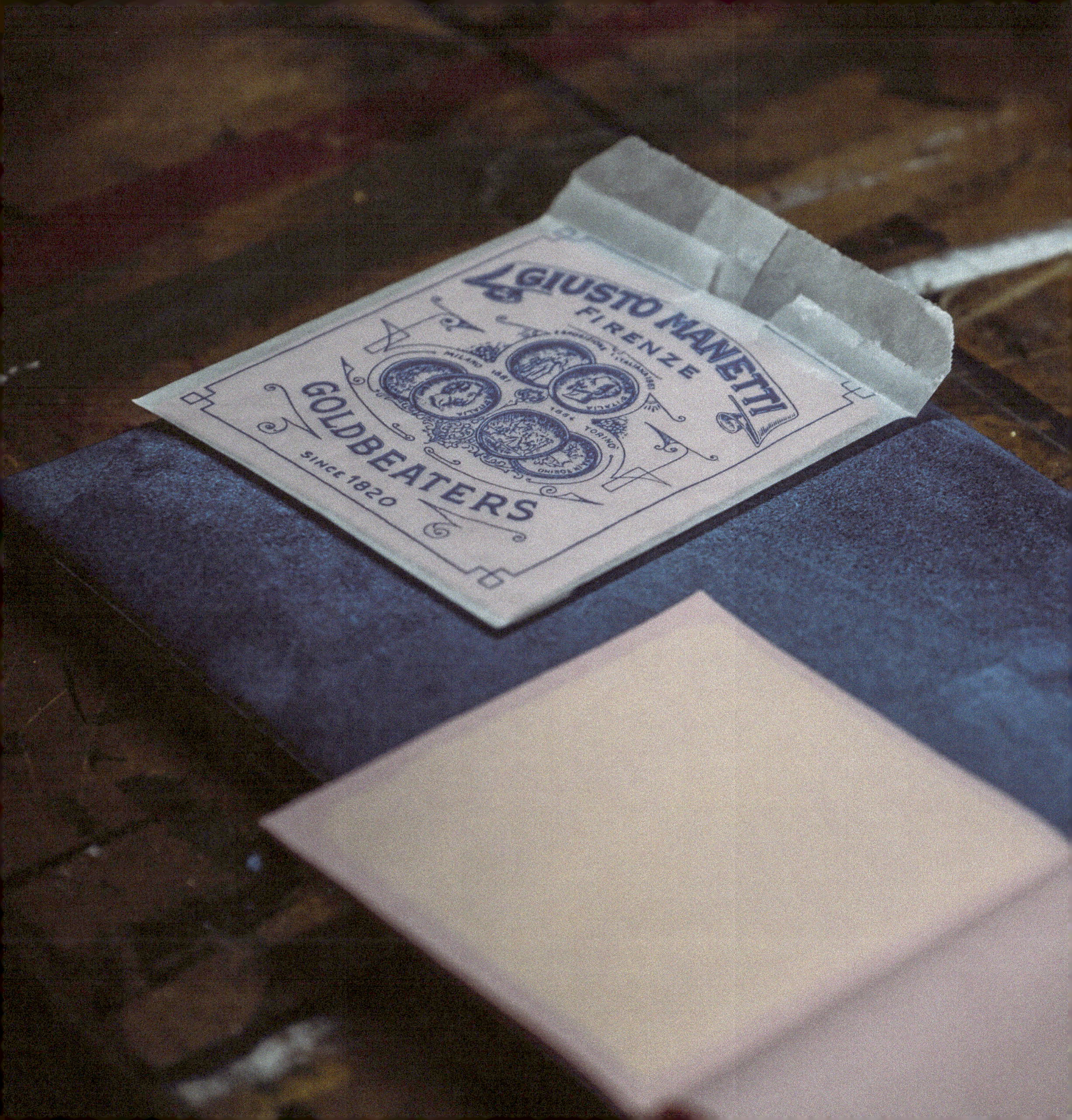
GIUSTO MANETTI
FIRENZE
GOLDBEATERS
SINCE 1820
MILANO
TORINO

examine your beliefs.

art is communication.
examine who you are and why
and you will be able to effectively
communicate through your work.

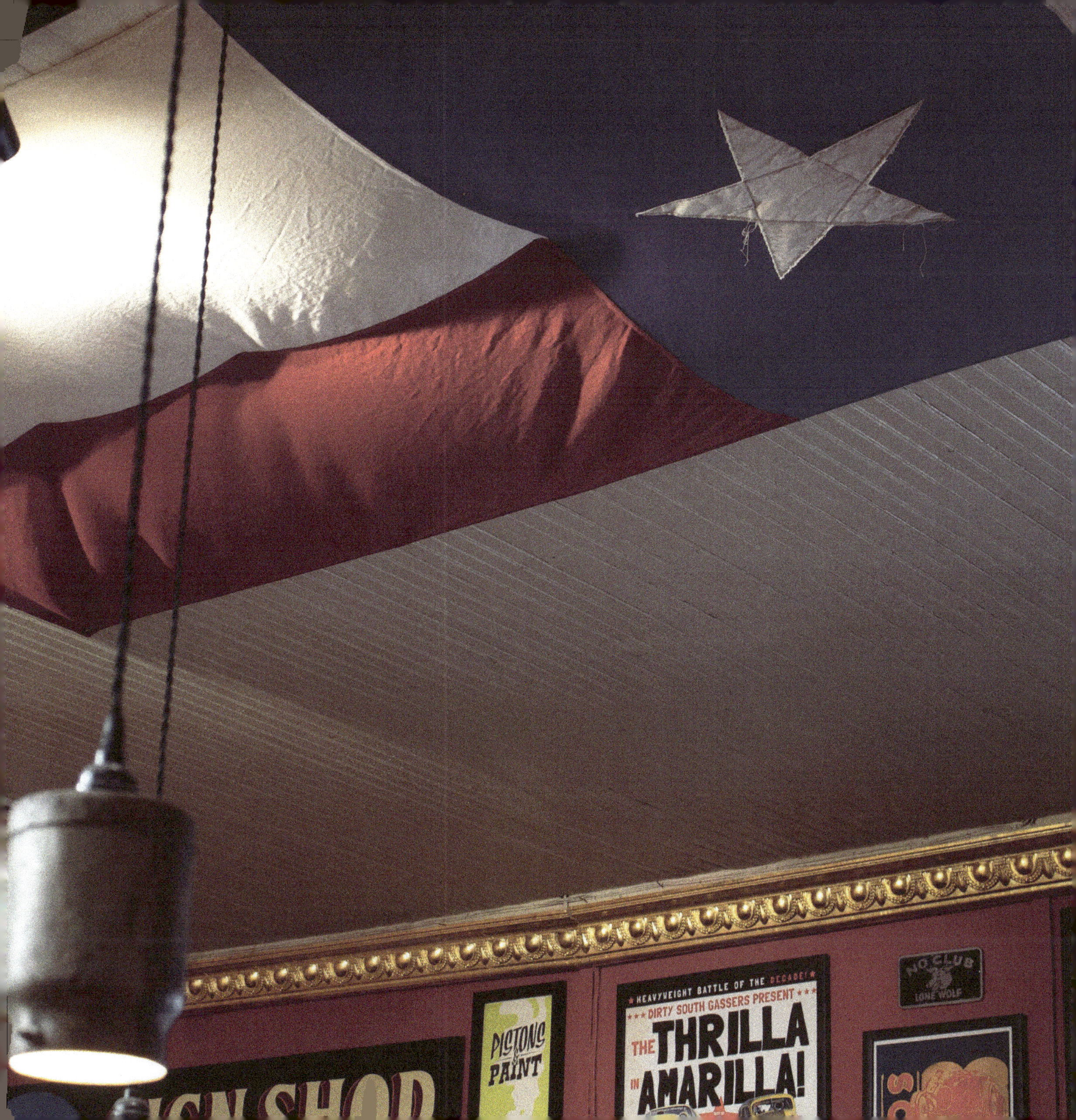

PISTONS & PAINT
HEAVYWEIGHT BATTLE OF THE DECADE!
DIRTY SOUTH GASSERS PRESENT
THE THRILLA IN AMARILLA!
NO CLUB LONE WOLF
IGN SHOP

accept change.

we are in a constant state of change.
everything in nature changes.
accept change, embrace it.

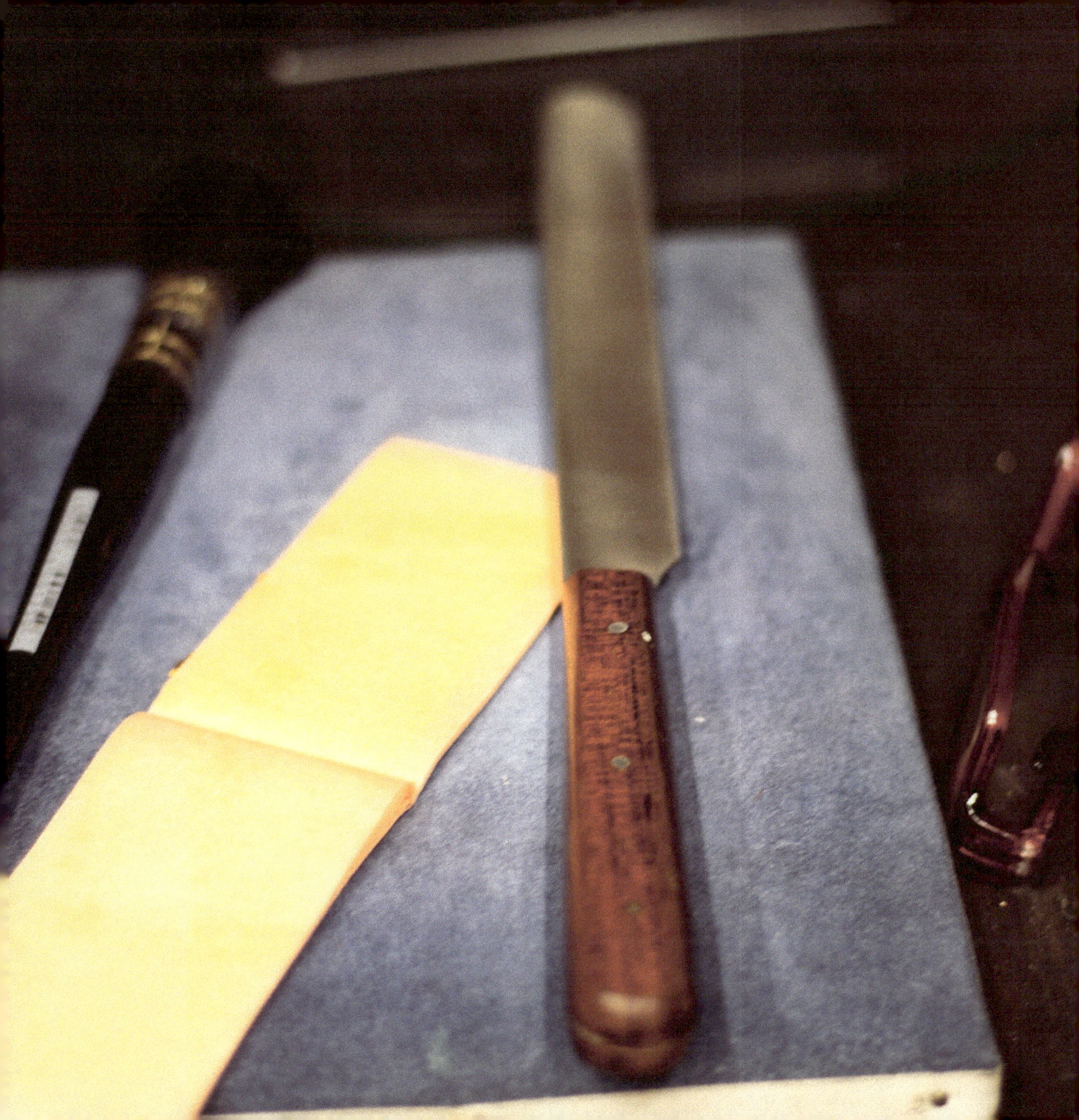

art is love.

the countless hours learning how to
express yourself and sharing that with
others is an incredible act of love.

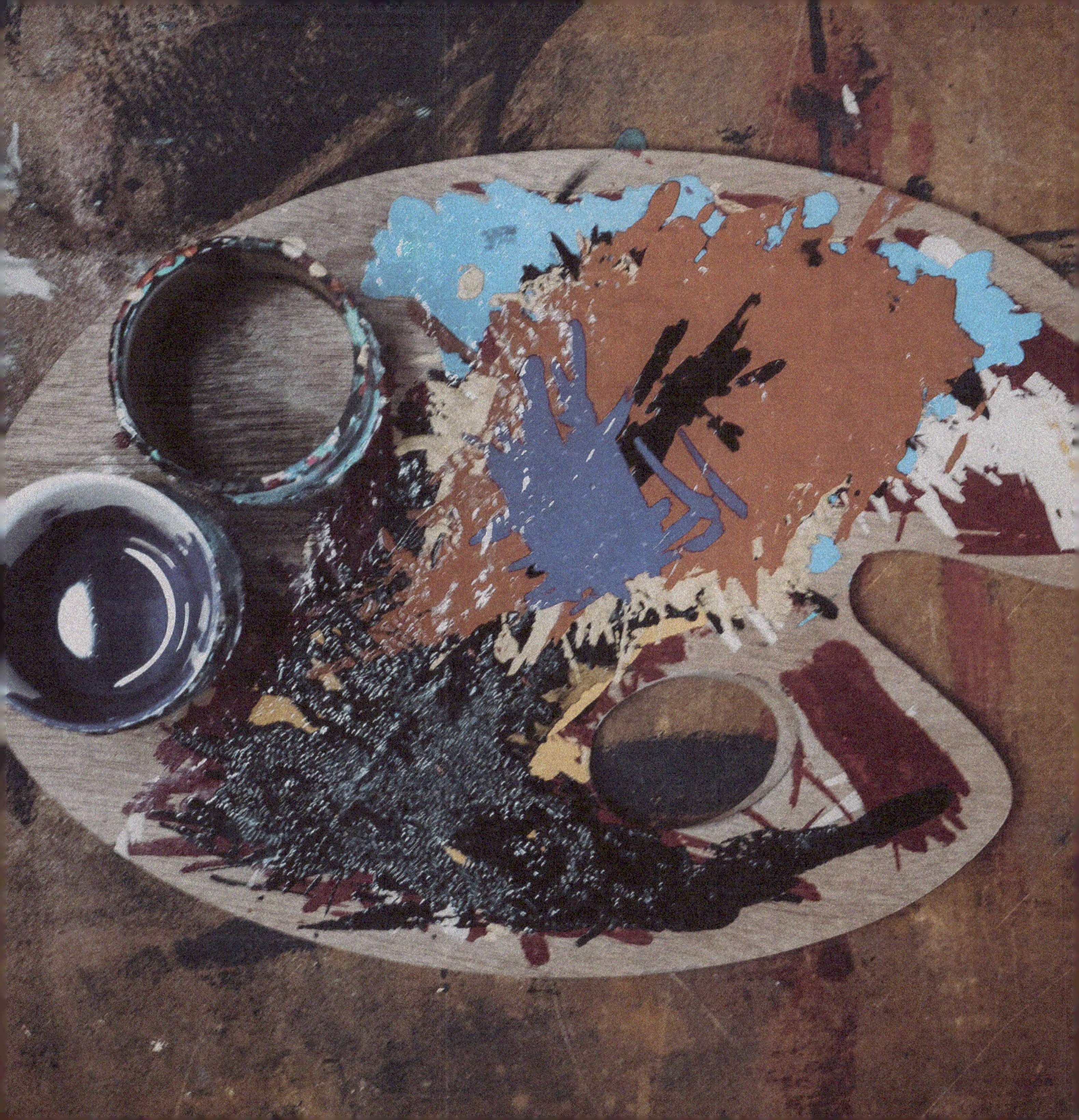

visualize.

visualize your work and move towards
it little by little.
tiny streams can alter a landscape
as long as they continue to flow.

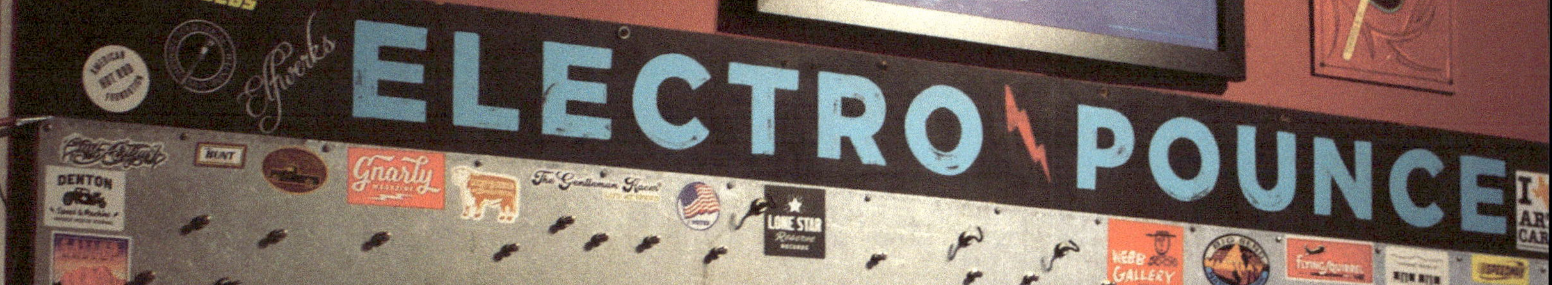
ELECTRO POUNCE

go dormant.

allow yourself to be
creatively dormant at times.
sometimes your creativity
decides to sleep.

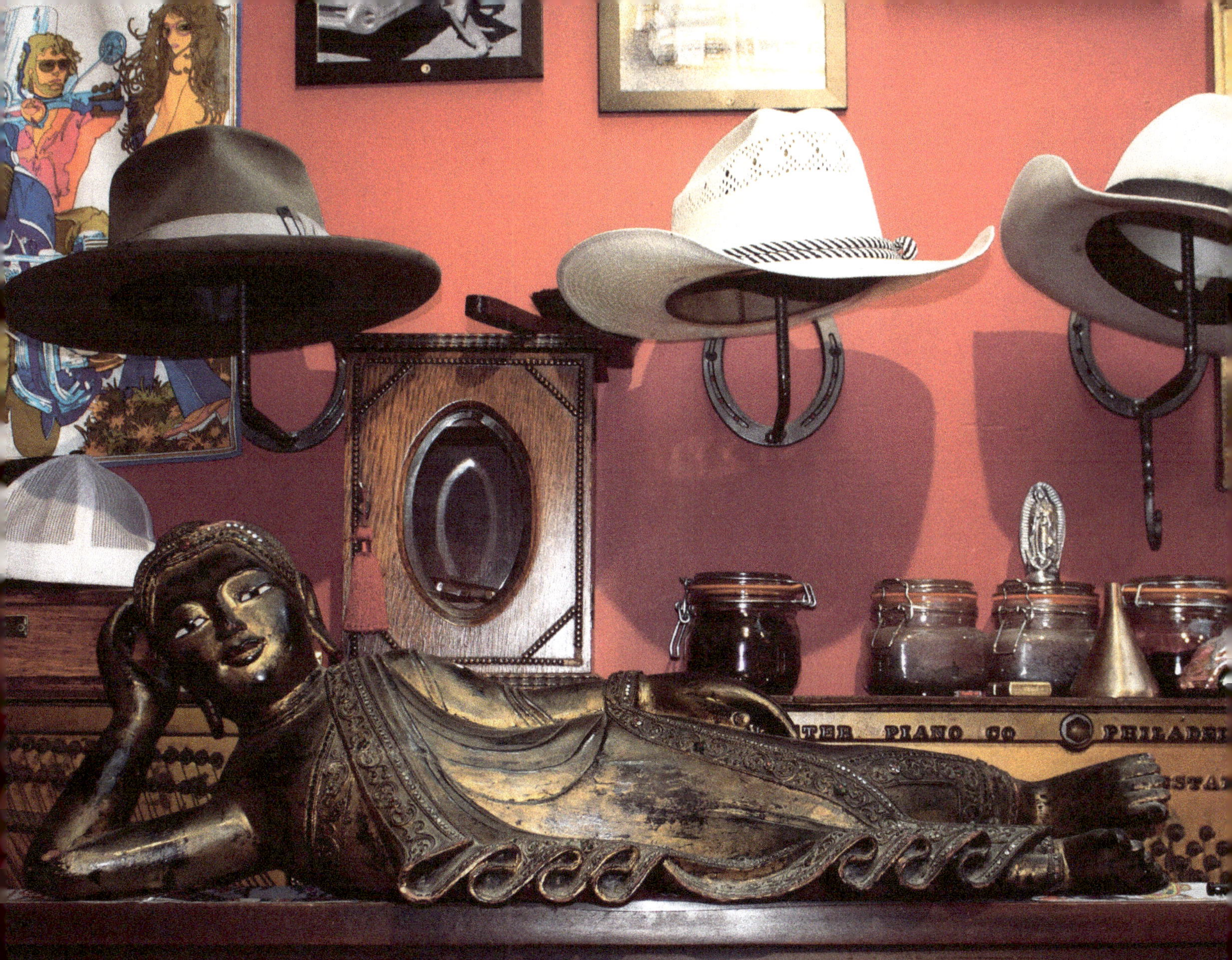
M GONNA TURN AND FACE THE M
THE MUSIC OF THE SPHERES"
VAN MORRISON

be fearless.

the more you use your voice,
the closer you will be to
becoming fearless.

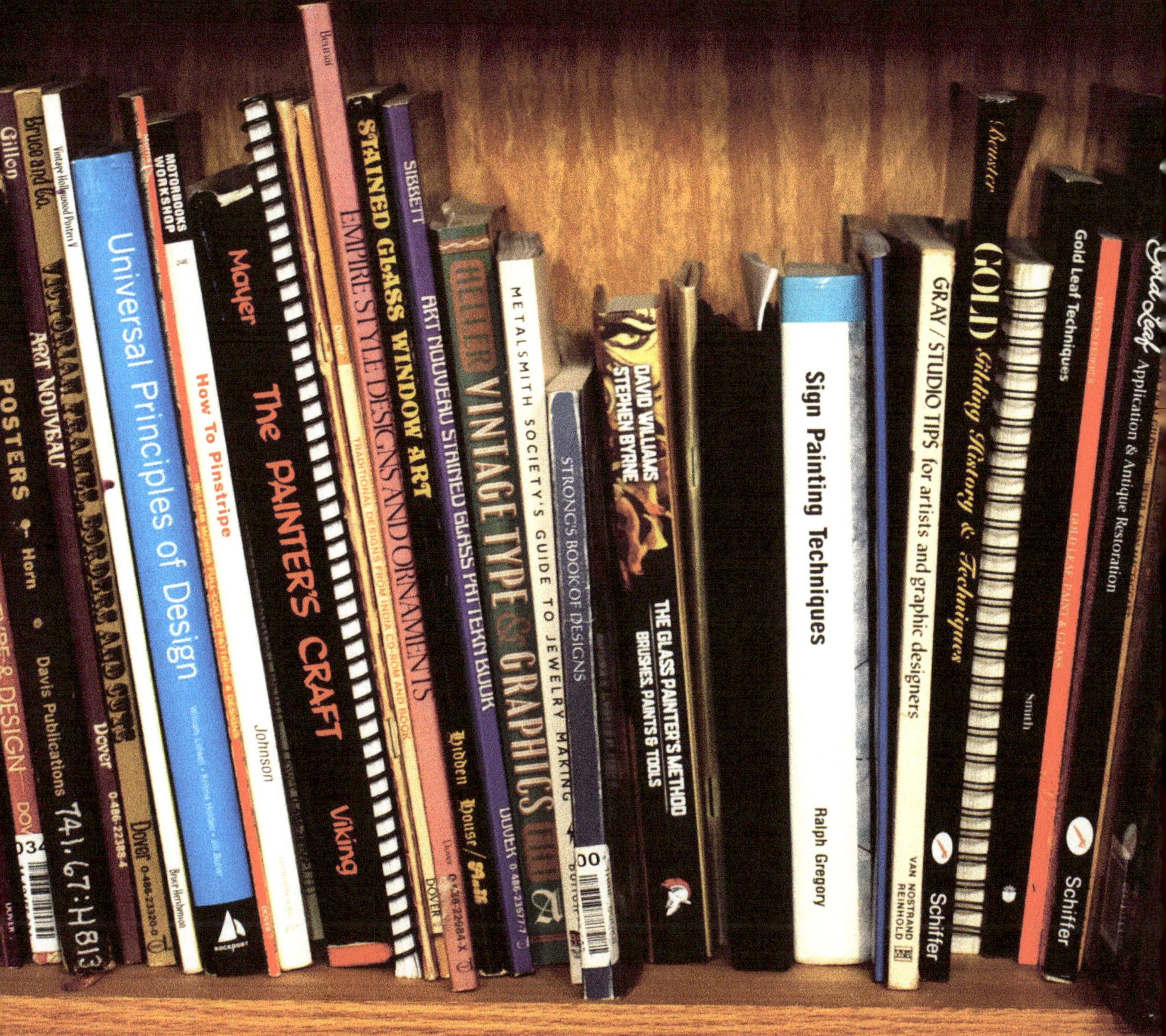

Gillon
Bruce and Co.
Vintage Hollywood Posters V
VICTORIAN FRAMES, BORDERS AND CUTS
ART NOUVEAU
Davis Publications
POSTERS
Horn
TYPE & DESIGN
DOV
MOTORBOOKS WORKSHOP
Universal Principles of Design
Dover
0-486-22386-4
Mayer
How To Pinstripe
The PAINTER'S CRAFT
Johnson
STAINED GLASS
SIBBETT
EMPIRE STYLE DESIGNS AND ORNAMENTS
WINDOW ART
ART NOUVEAU STAINED GLASS PATTERN BOOK
Viking
VINTAGE TYPE & GRAPHICS
METALSMITH SOCIETY'S GUIDE TO JEWELRY MAKING
STRONG'S BOOK OF DESIGNS
DAVID WILLIAMS
STEPHEN BYRNE
THE GLASS PAINTER'S METHOD
BRUSHES, PAINTS & TOOLS
Sign Painting Techniques
Ralph Gregory
GRAY / STUDIO TIPS for artists and graphic designers
VAN NOSTRAND REINHOLD
GOLD
Gilding History & Techniques
Smith
Schiffer
Gold Leaf Techniques
Gold Leaf
Application & Antique Restoration
Schiffer
Brewster

be patient.

development of ideas and
techniques take time.
breathe.

work hard.

it is a wonderful pursuit to work
hard for what you love most.
work hard at developing

your voice.

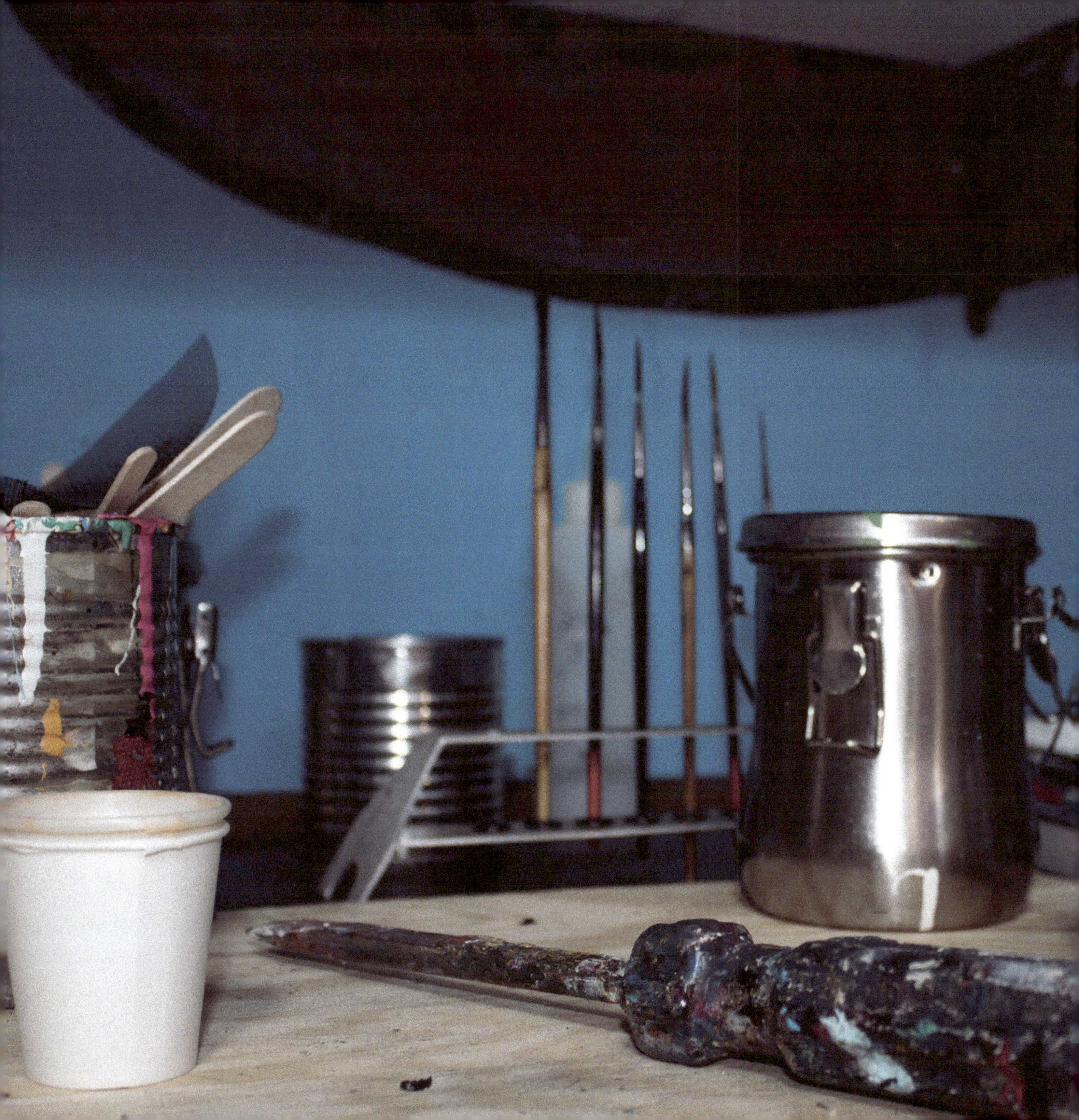

develop grace.

be patient with other people struggling to
find their voice, a frustrated person
can seem really unreasonable.
develop grace in your work and life.

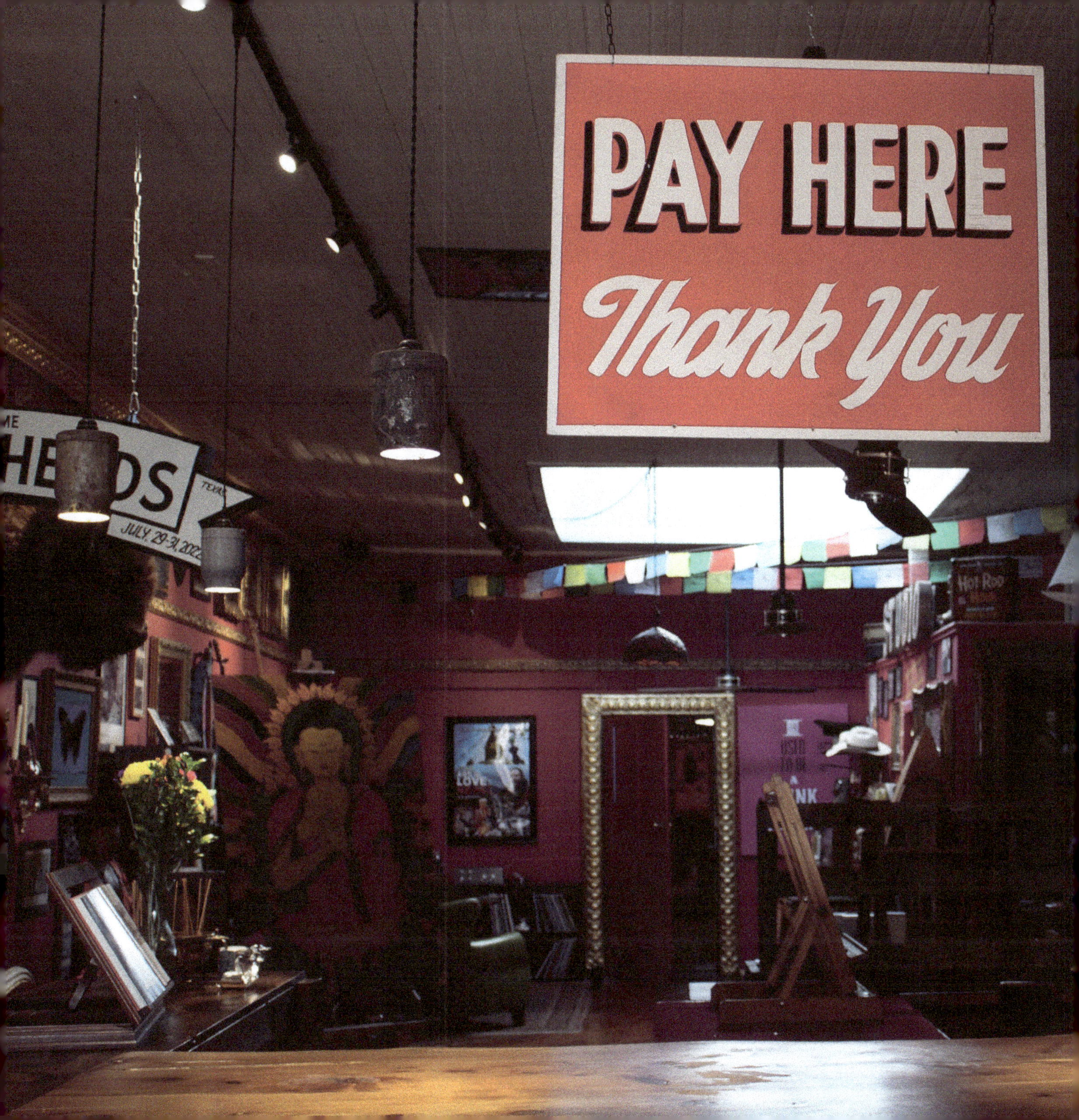

PAY HERE
Thank You
HEADS
TEXAS
JULY 29-31, 2022
LOVE
Hot Rod

have insight.

you will never fully understand
the work you create.
neither will anyone else.

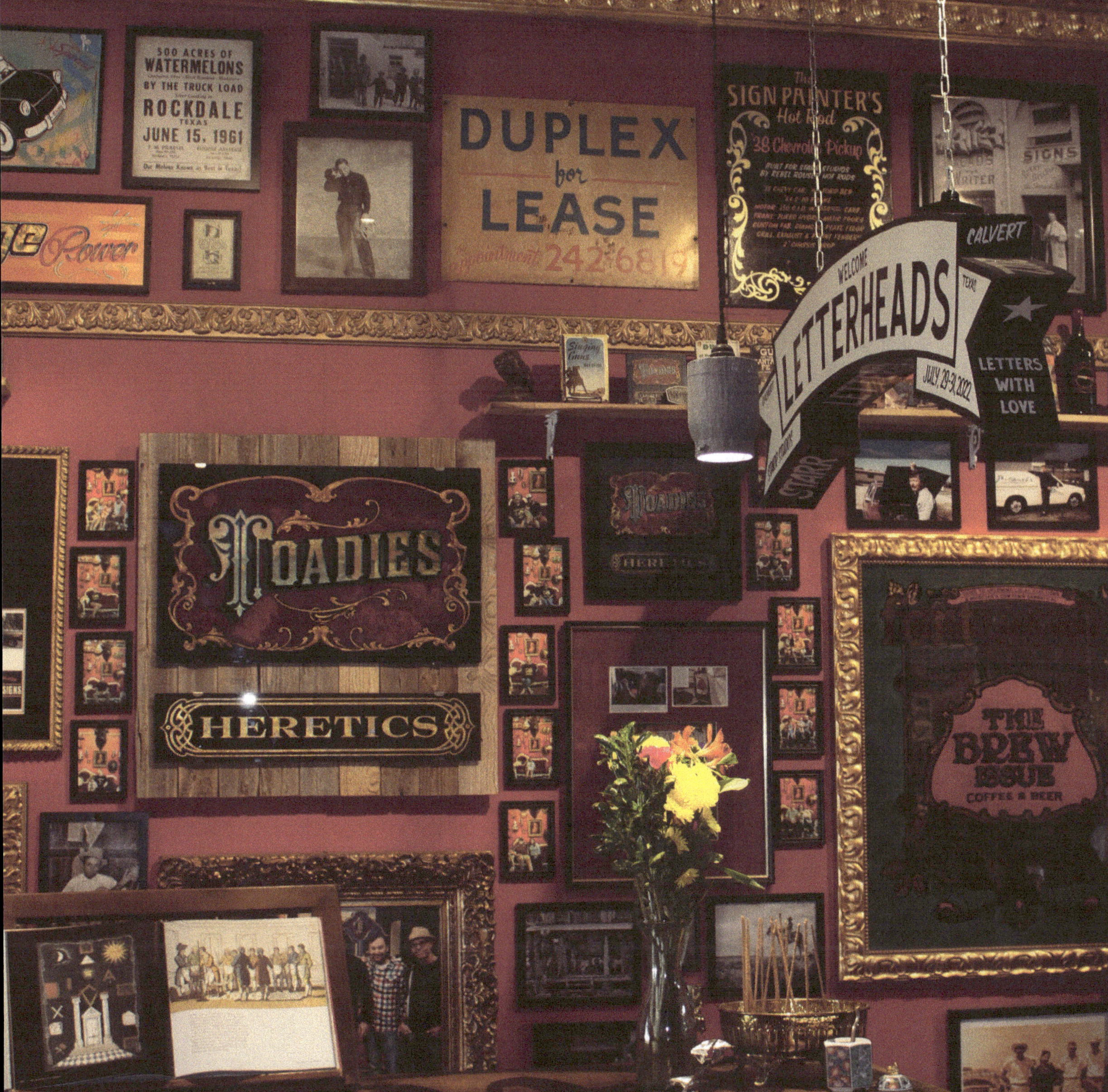
500 ACRES OF
WATERMELONS
BY THE TRUCK LOAD
ROCKDALE
TEXAS
JUNE 15, 1961
DUPLEX
for
LEASE
Apartment 242-6819
The
SIGN PAINTER'S
Hot Rod
38 Chevrolet Pickup
SIGNS
WRITER
Power
WELCOME
LETTERHEADS
CALVERT
TEXAS
JULY 29-31 2022
LETTERS
WITH
LOVE
STARR
ROADIES
HERETICS
ROADIES
HERE U.S.A
THE
BREW
ISSUE
COFFEE & BEER

be here now.

today is an awesome day.
you are miles from where you started
and you are on the path to greater things.

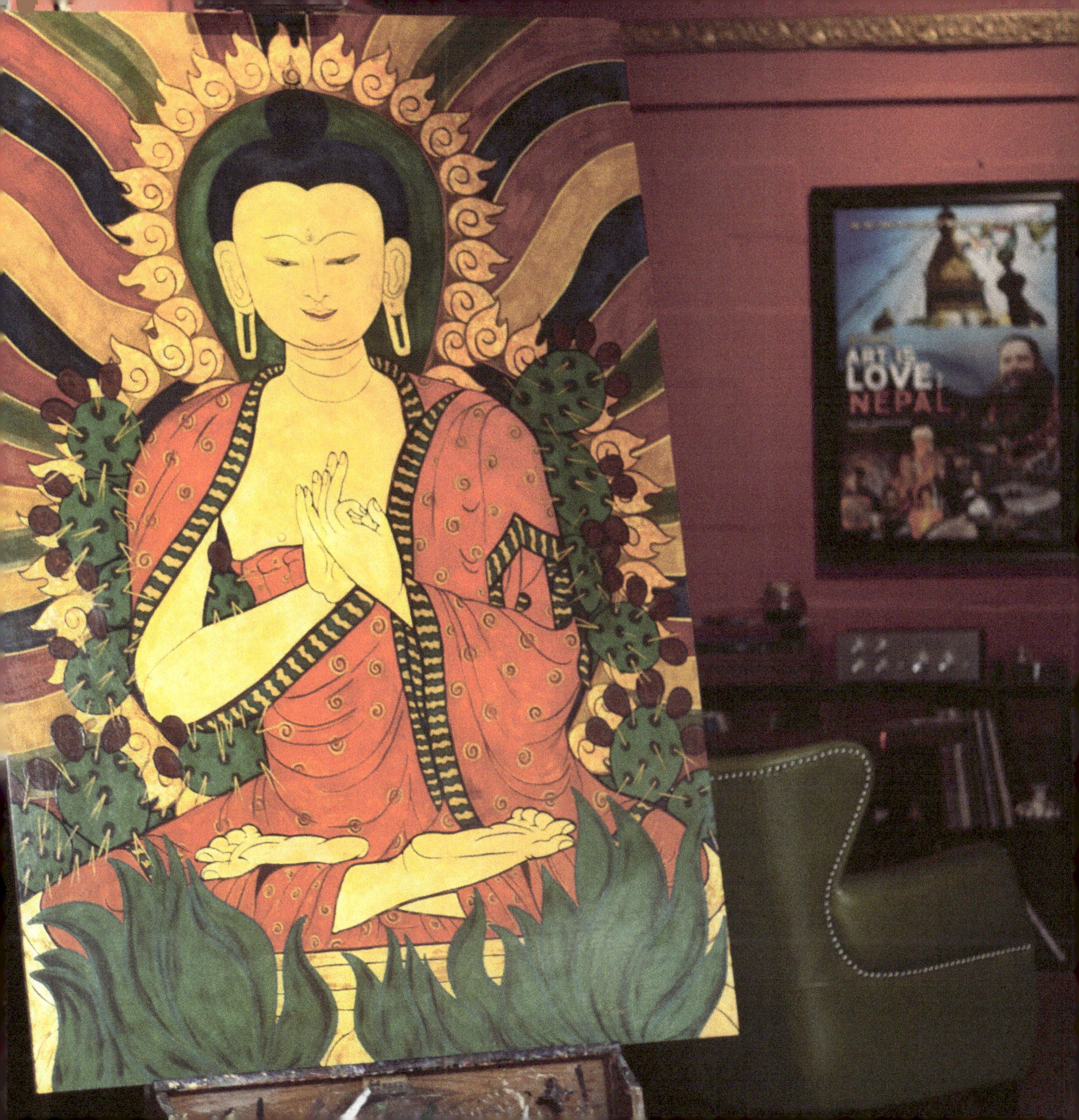
ART IS
LOVE
NEPAL

avoid envy.

do not envy the success of other artists,
they have different burdens
to carry because of it.

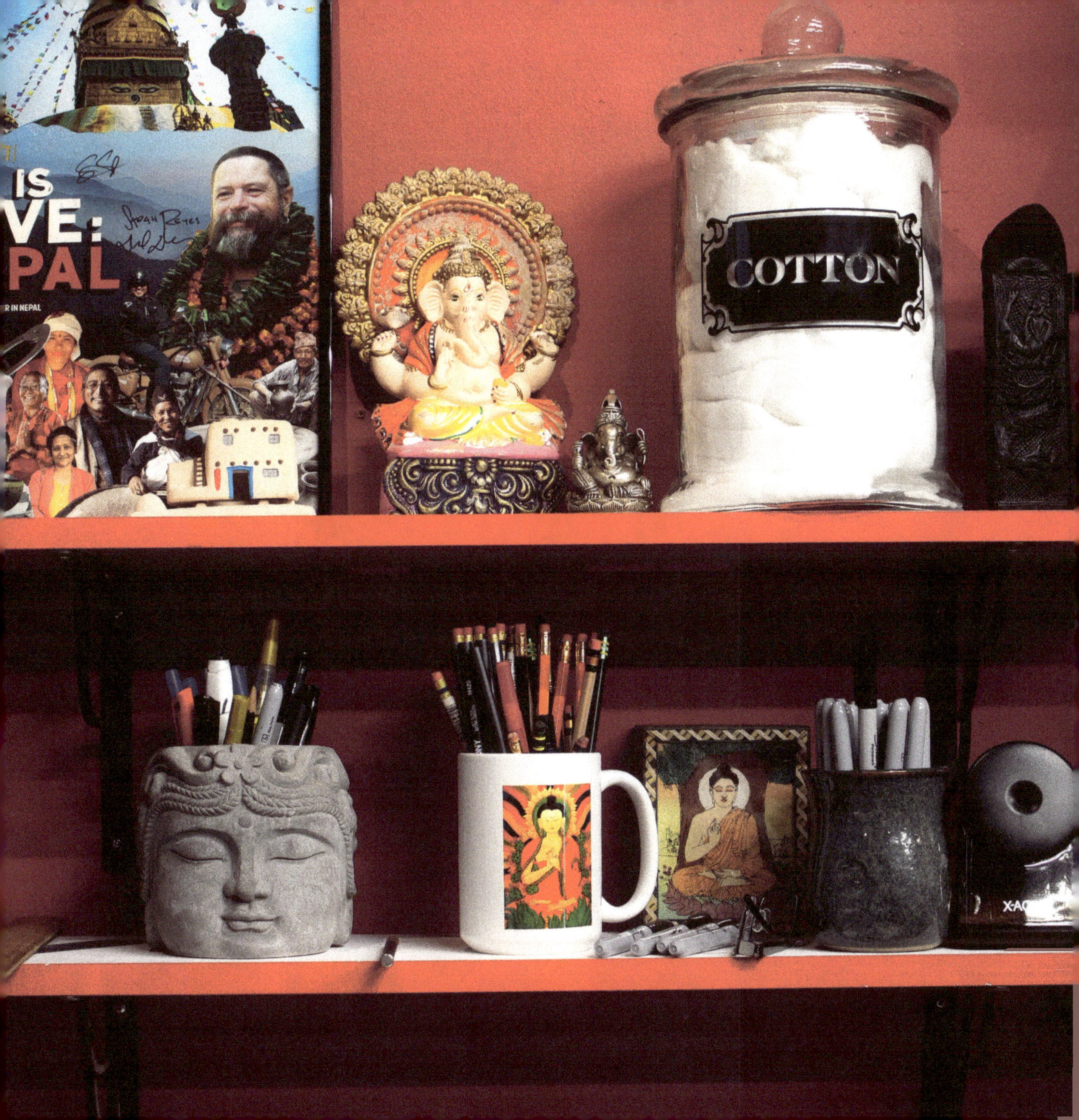

IS
VE:
PAL
R IN NEPAL

COTTON

be comfortable being unique.

represent yourself on the outside
with who you are on the inside.
never attempt to imprison
your true self.

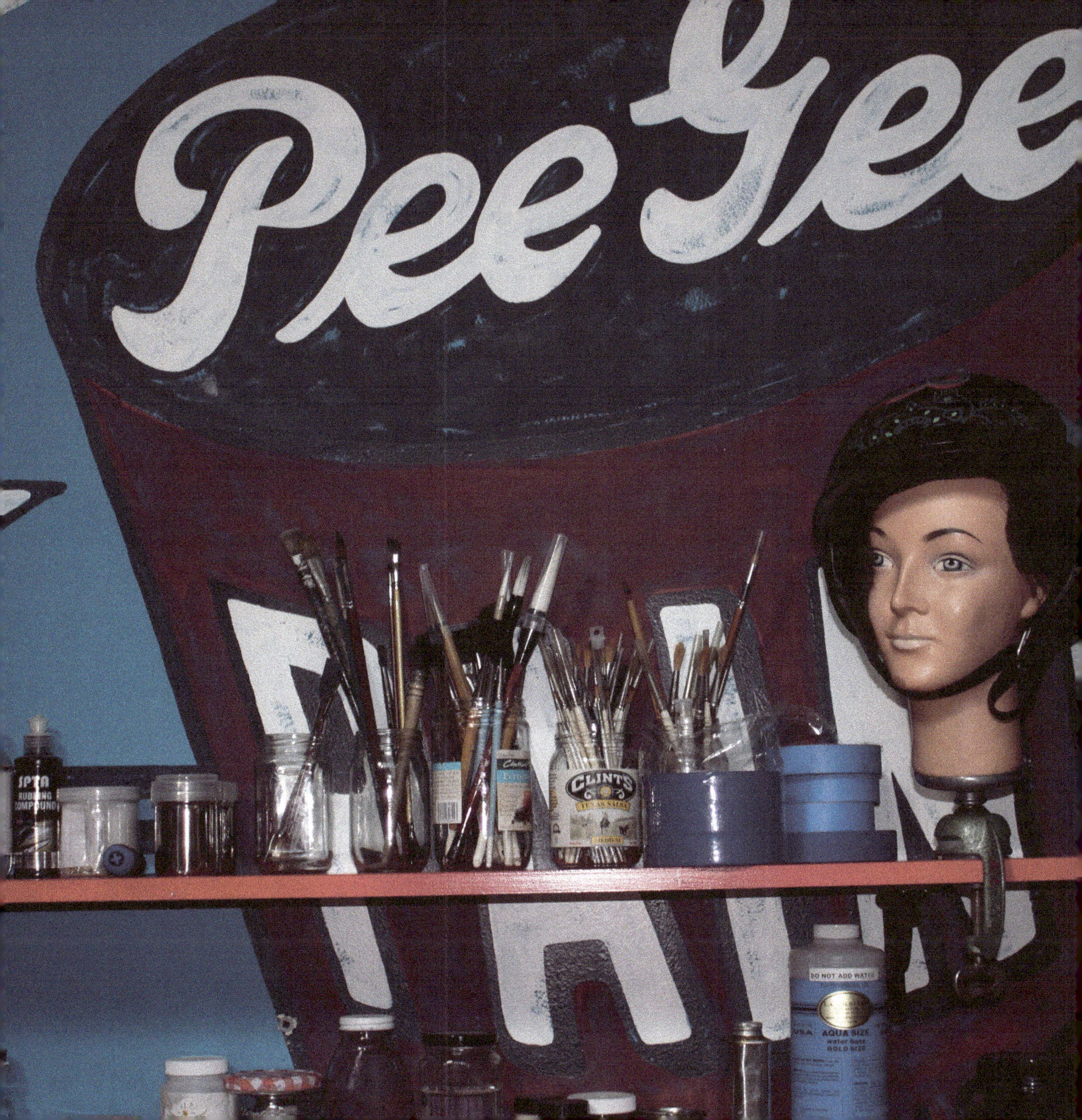
Pee Gee
SPRA
RUBBING
COMPOUND
CLINT'S
DO NOT ADD WATER
USA
AQUA SIZE
water-base
GOLD SIZE

accept your mortality.

embrace the concept of your own ending.
it is the only way
you will actually start
living life
to its fullest.

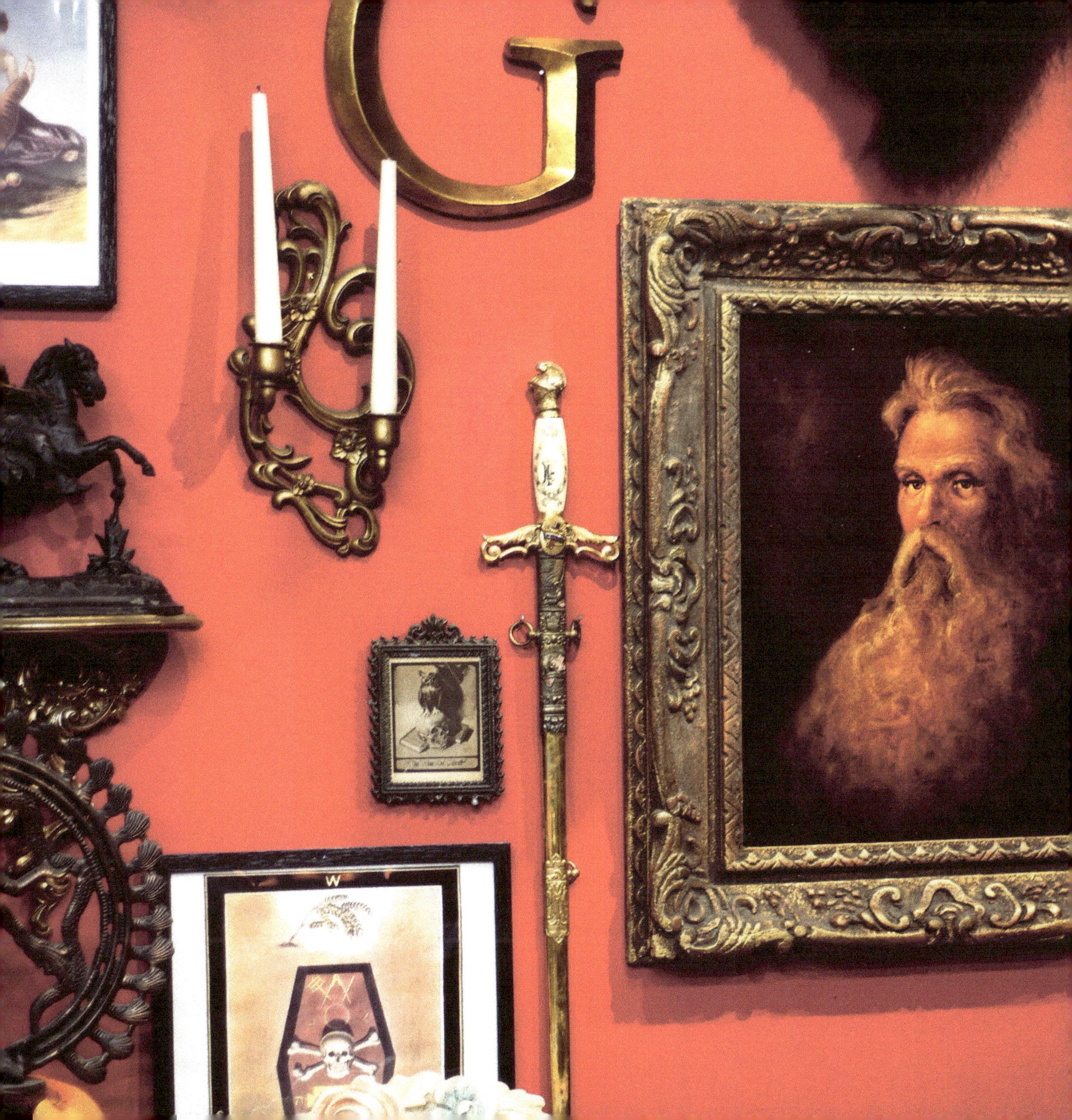

be the temple keeper.

make your home
a temple of love and beauty.
keep the wolves on the outside.

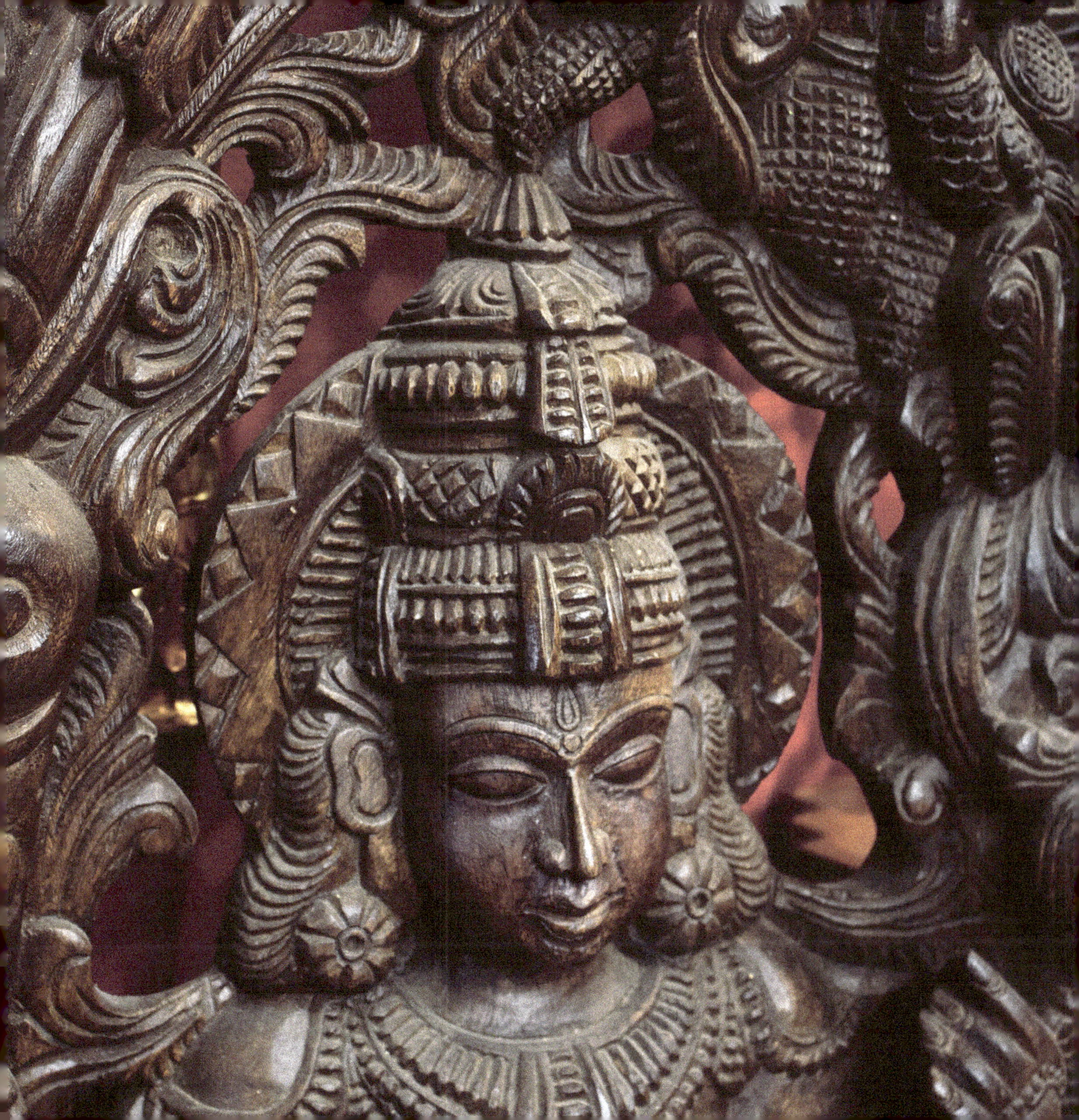

learn refinement.

approach your work
like a good bottle of wine.
the moment the bottle is opened
all the stages of its creation
come together
to meet up as one fantastic
experience.

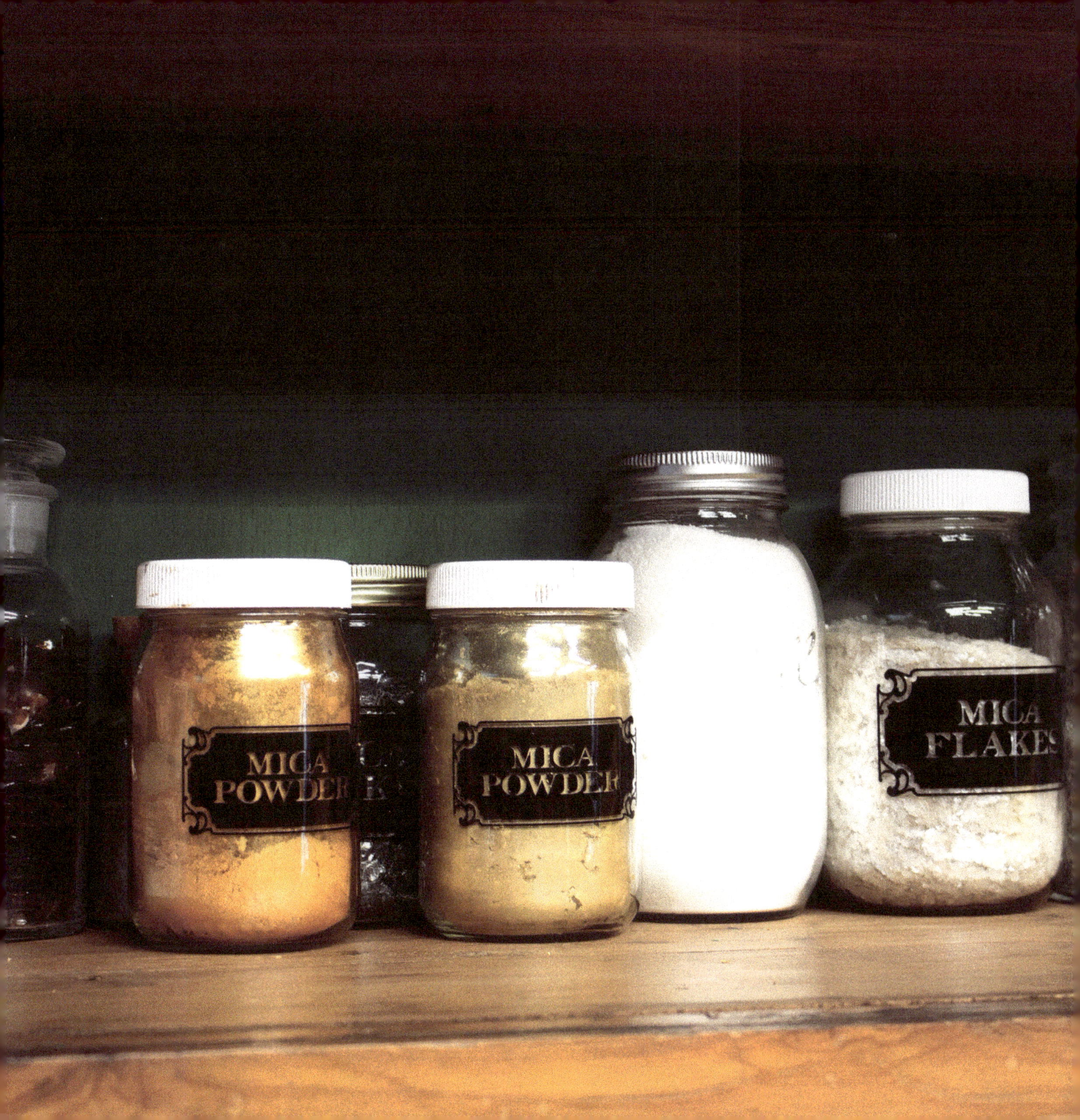

MICA
POWDER
MICA
POWDER
MICA
FLAKES

play like a child.

growing up is a lousy goal,
never stop playing.

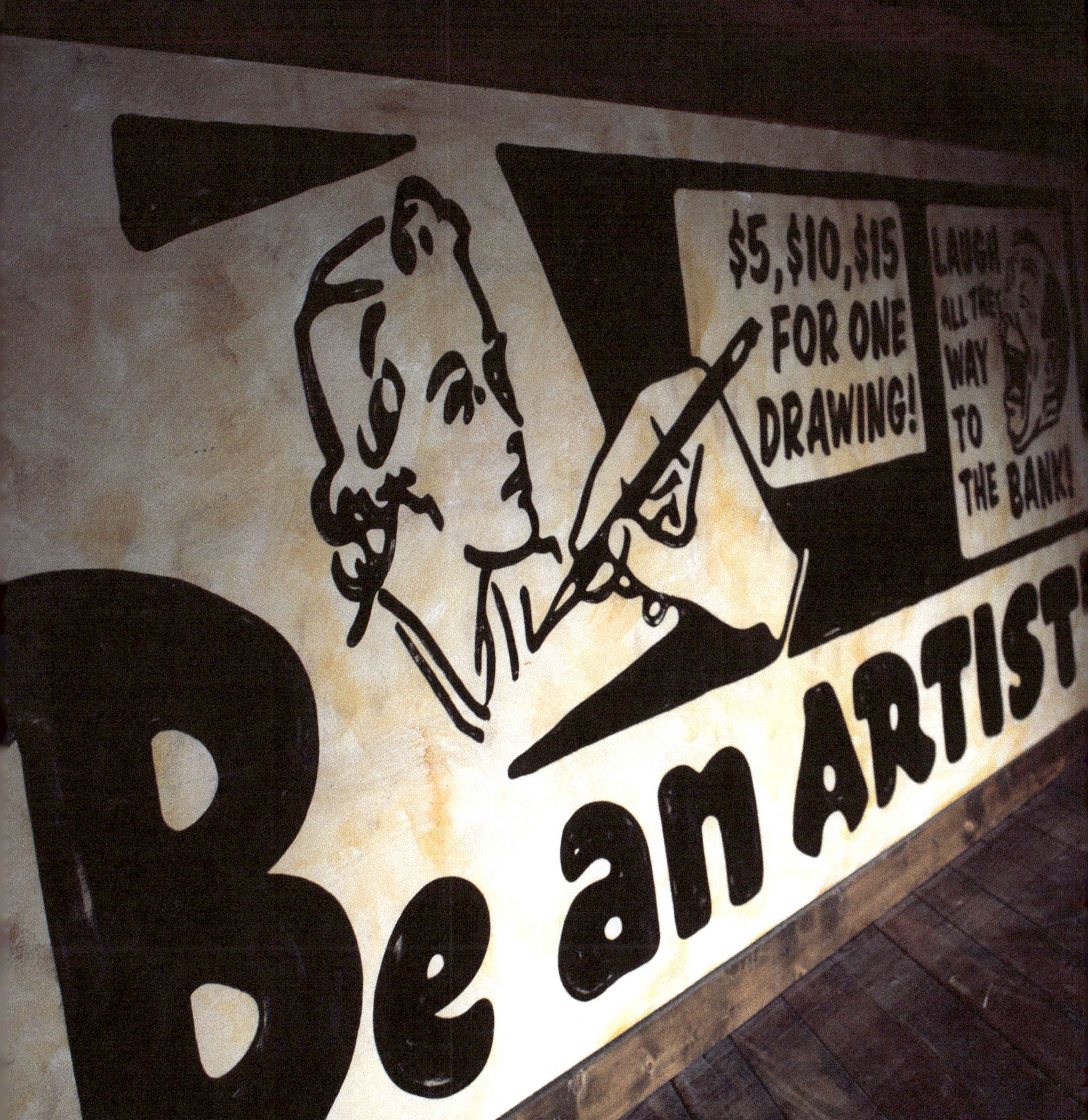

Be an ARTIST!
$5, $10, $15 FOR ONE DRAWING!
LAUGH ALL THE WAY TO THE BANK!

keep beauty in front of you.

place fresh flowers on your table
once a week to remind you
that beauty is effortless in nature.

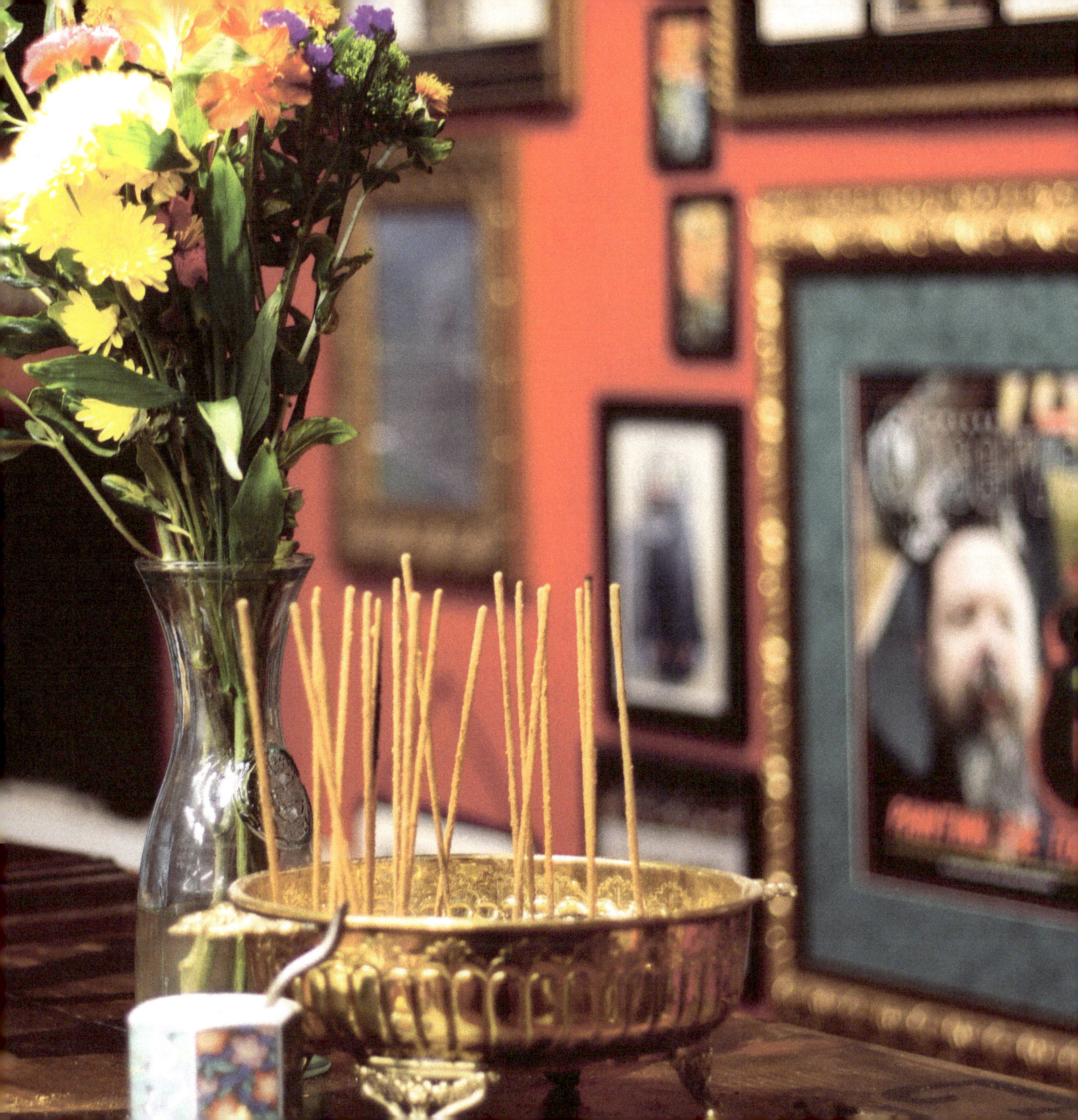

use the pain.

rise above the hurt
and heartache of your past.
embrace the opportunity
to create something
beautiful from it.

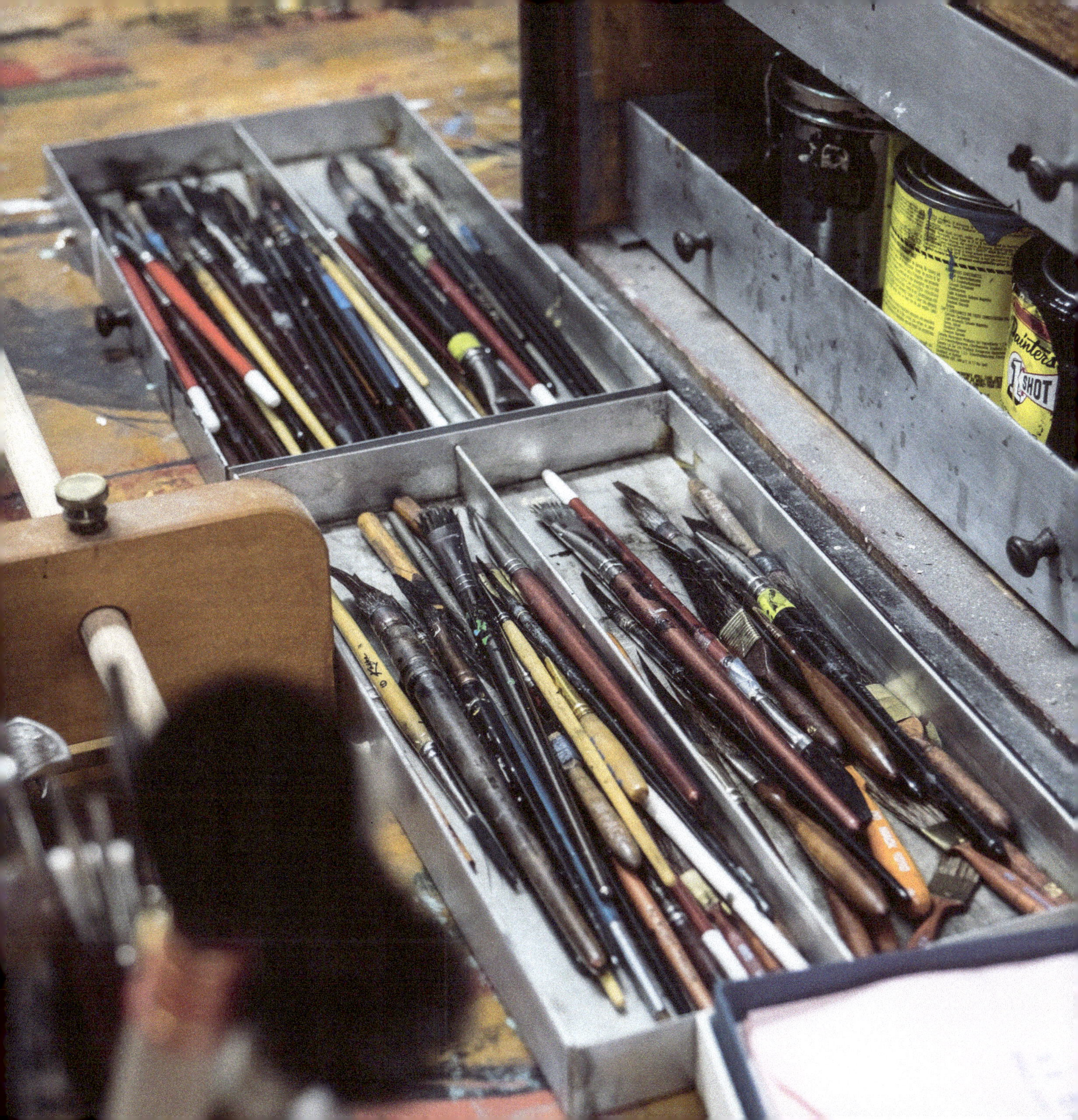

find the flow.

if you have to force
any aspect of your work,
your approach needs revisiting.
your work should
develop effortlessly.

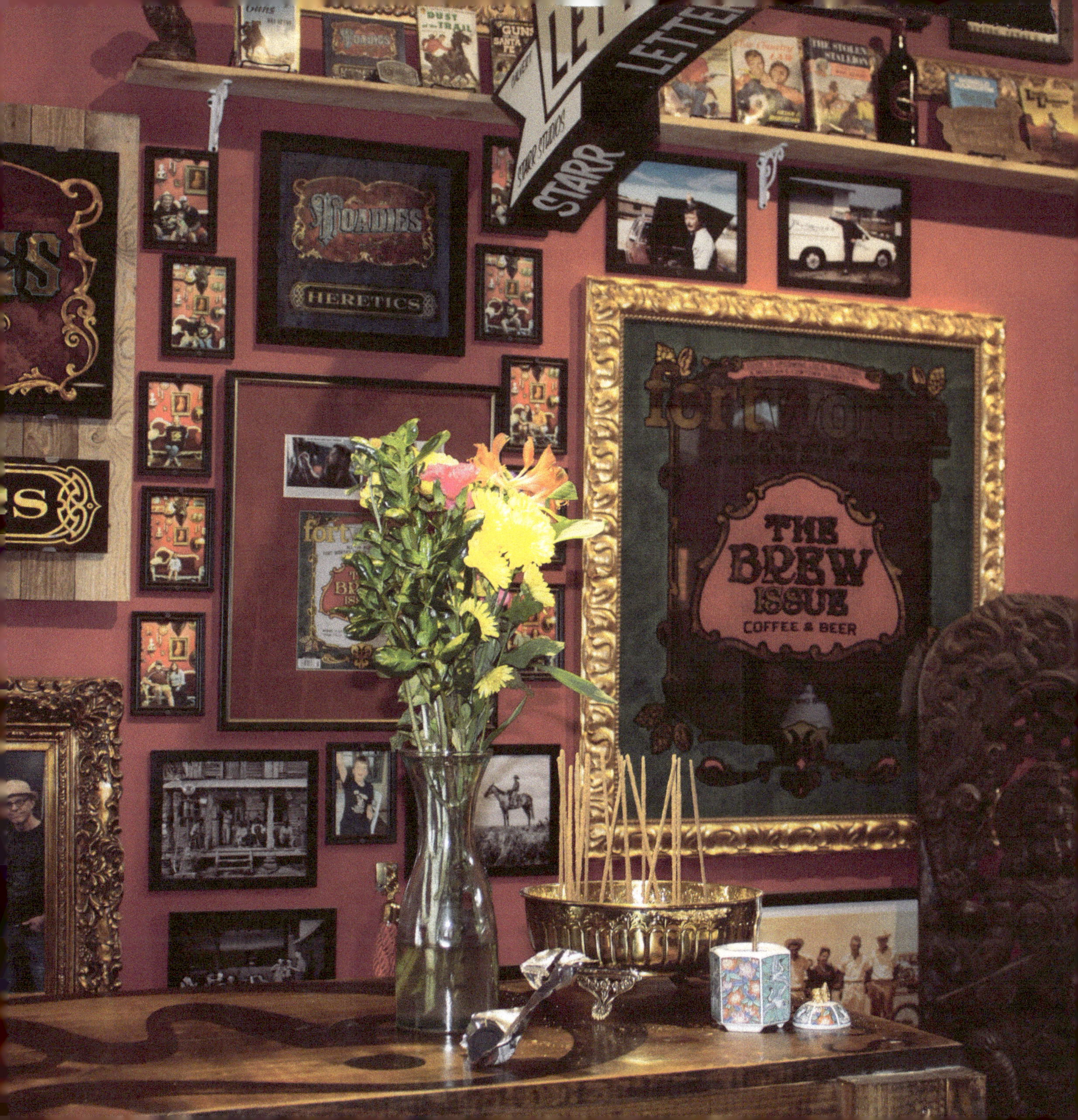
ROADIES
HERETICS
STARR
LETTE
THE
BREW
ISSUE
COFFEE & BEER

know when to stop.

when your inner voice
tells you to stop working
on something, it is finished.

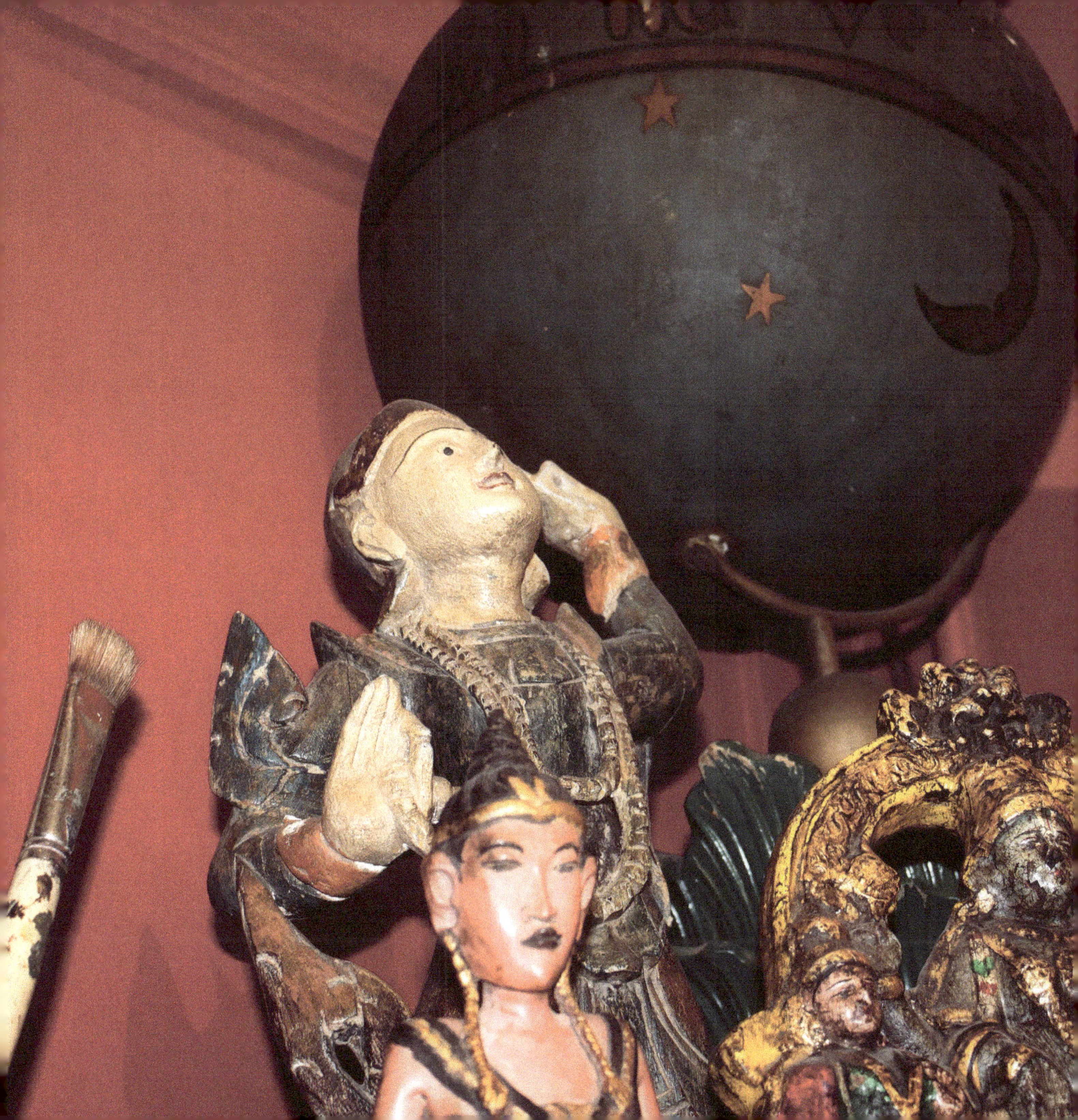

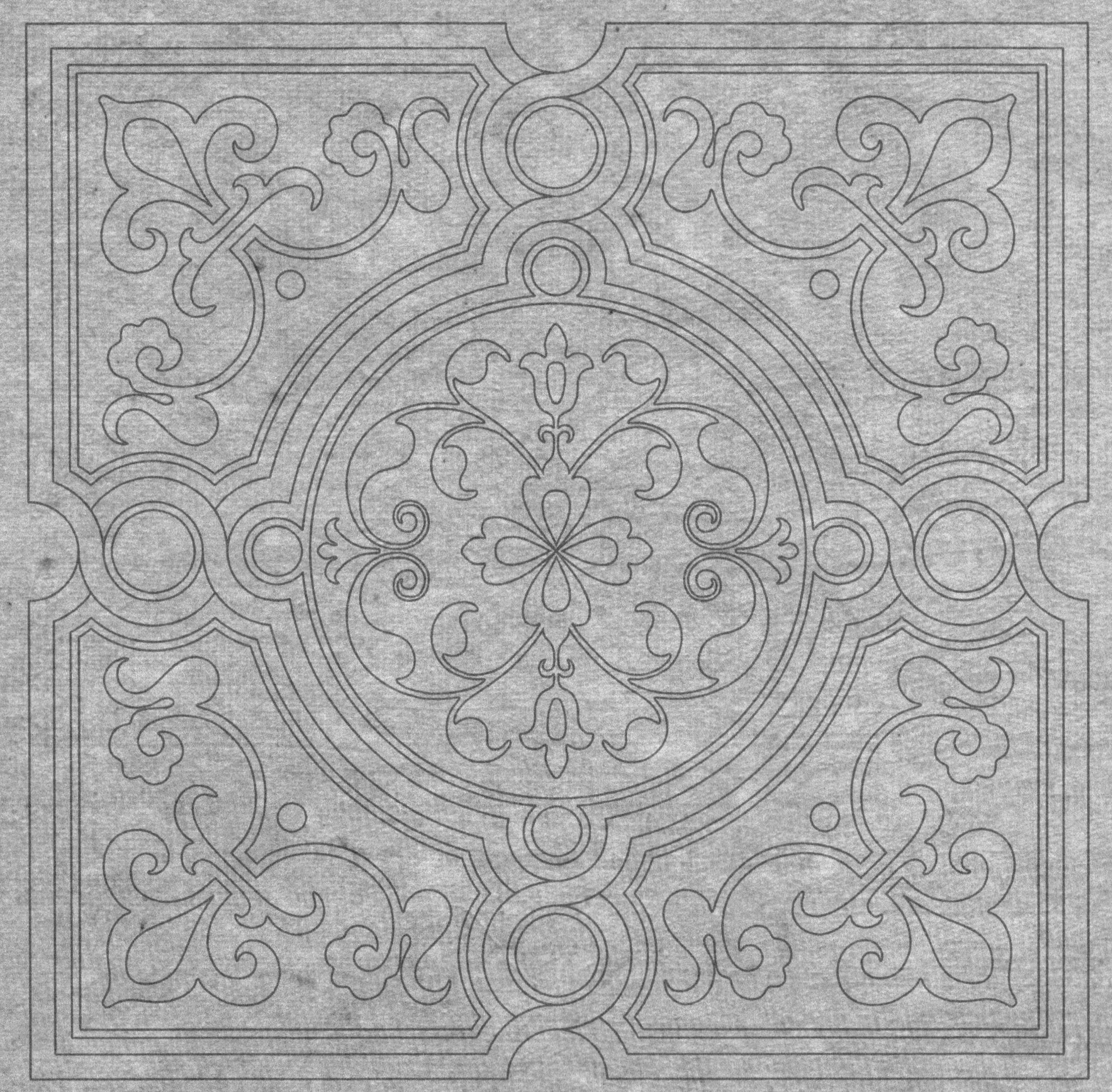

* 9 7 9 8 8 6 9 2 1 9 2 9 9 *